Clothed
with
Gladness

Clothed with
Gladness
The Story of St. Clare

Sister Mary St. Paul, P.C.C.

Our Sunday Visitor Publishing Division
Our Sunday Visitor, Inc.
Huntington, Indiana 46750

Our Sunday Visitor Publishing Division
Our Sunday Visitor, Inc.
200 Noll Plaza
Huntington, IN 46750

LCCN: 99-75025
ISBN: 087973-285-7

Cover Design by Tyler Ottinger
Illustrations by Sister Mary Veronica, P.C.C.
Edited by Lisa Grote

Dedication

This small life of Saint Clare is gratefully dedicated to
the cherished memory of

Father David Temple, O.F.M.,

an outstanding Franciscan Friar of the
Santa Barbara Province.

It was through his enthusiasm, scholarship, and wholly
genuine Franciscan spirit that the "fire" we call Francis
and Clare caught flame and came to life for many
Franciscans, including this author.

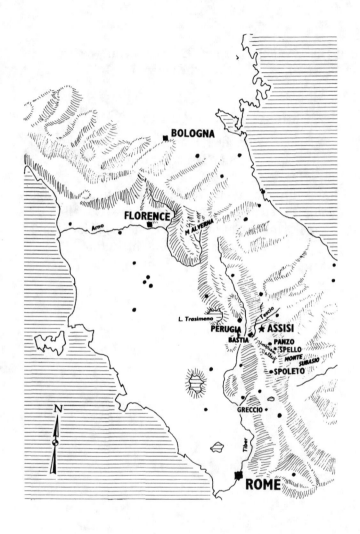

BOLOGNA

FLORENCE

Arno

M ALVERNA

L. Trasimeno

Tescio

PERUGIA ★ ASSISI

BASTIA

PANZO

Umbrian Valley SPELLO

MONTE SUBASIO

SPOLETO

N

GRECCIO

Tiber

ROME

Table of Contents

Foreword

Clothed with Gladness

As anyone familiar with Franciscan history can tell you, only one person ever really followed Saint Francis perfectly. That was Saint Clare of Assisi. Saint Francis's vocation was so absolute in all its details that even the greatest of his spiritual followers lived with modifications to his rule, giving themselves as completely to God as he did, but without the poetic literalness of his vocation as a disciple of Jesus Christ. Down the centuries marvelous sons and daughters of Saint Francis, unlike their founder, have lived in modest buildings, have had books, and have eaten regular meals. In modern times they have even flown in airplanes. Saint Maximilian Kolbe, the towering Franciscan of this age, even ran an airport as part of his publishing apostolate. Great sanctity as a Franciscan does not seem to have required the literal following of the Saint, who was so unworldly that he is often described by the mysterious and daunting adjective *seraphic*. The secret of the Franciscan saints is that they sought to emulate his inner poverty and to live with as much material frugality as their vocations would realistically permit.

But there was one who went all the way along the road to perfection with Saint Francis, and that was Saint Clare. Although she is not so well known as the *Poverello*, Saint Clare, in her own way, is the Franciscan mystic *par excellence.* What is her special charism? What makes Saint Clare so obviously herself, and not simply a reflection of Saint Francis? She is not an ecstatic who reshapes the history of the Church, like Saint Catherine of Siena.

She is not the psychological and spiritual genius whom we meet in the writings of Saint Teresa of Ávila. She more closely resembles Saint Thérèse of Lisieux in totality of her consecration. But there is something eminently medieval about Saint Clare, as there is something quintessentially modern about the newest Doctor of the Church.

I would hesitate even to give a precise name to the poverty and simplicity of spirit possessed by Saint Clare, but whatever it may best be called, I think that Sister Mary Saint Paul has captured it in these biographical meditations. This beautiful book is not a scholarly historical study or a partly fictionalized biography. It is in fact a series of vignettes, like frescoes or stained-glass windows, that seem to me to depict so well the ideals and life of Saint Clare of Assisi. The sketches by Sister Mary Veronica in their simplicity are the perfect accompaniment to the meditations of the author.

For some readers, both Catholic and non-Catholic, this book will also serve as an unexpected introduction to the life of contemplative nuns. Since I was a teenager, I have been visiting contemplative nuns, and in recent decades I have given retreats to several houses of nuns — Benedictines, Carmelites, Dominicans, Sacramentines, Visitadines, and of course the Poor Clares. I have also given retreats to some of the newer communities of contemplative nuns, including the Adorers of the Precious Blood, the Sisters of the Cross, the Sisters of Bethlehem, the contemplative Missionaries of Charity, and the Servants of the Holy Spirit. Each community that genuinely observes its charism leaves you with a different sense. While it is often difficult to identify precisely what the different charisms are, they seem to be a combination of ideals, history, customs, and how the goals of the spiritual life are lived out. If you are not fortunate enough to have contemplative religious among your friends, *Clothed with Gladness* will introduce you to the cloistered life in general and to the specific spirituality of the Order of Saint Clare.

To get the most out of this book, you must read it with prayer, silence, and recollection, and no more than one chapter at a time. You will come to know one of the most dedicated of all Christ's followers of the last two thousand years. At the same time you will obtain an insight into the lives of cloistered contemplative nuns, who are less known and appreciated than they should be, but whose lives of selfless prayer and spiritual efforts provide astonishing but unseen graces for the Church and for the whole world.

— Father Benedict J. Groeschel, C.F.R.

Preface

Psalm 30:12 reads: "You took off my sackcloth and clothed me with gladness." This applies perfectly to Saint Clare of Assisi. Sister Mary St. Paul wants to help us to understand and experience how this came about.

To do this, she draws on biographical information about Saint Clare. However, she does not portray Saint Clare's holiness in the manner of a hagiographer; rather, she focuses on the action of the Holy Spirit. And so, we ponder the spiritual development in the life of Saint Clare.

Writing in language that is vivid and true-to-life, she shows sensitivity to Saint Clare's interior, spiritual motivations. Thus, the reader feels caught up in the story of a spiritual call which transformed the sackcloth of harsh living conditions into the garment of joy.

Her presentation is based on a thorough knowledge of Saint Clare's life and the history of her Order from its beginnings. Yet, along the more visible path of her life, the interior, spiritual path is constantly emerging. Sister Mary St. Paul also succeeds in conveying a continuity in the course of the conversion of Saint Clare's way of life — a life marked by poverty and deprivation — into one that brought encouragement and healing to others. This finally led Saint Clare to be transformed into Christ. He shines through her. He makes her pure and beautiful. This transformation is effected more and more in contemplation, in which she "puts on Christ" and thus wears interiorly the garment of his holiness and majesty.

— Father Herbert Schneider, O.F.M.

Introduction

Care has been taken in these pages to remain close to the historical facts about the life of Saint Clare. As may be expected, the distance of eight centuries has served to leave many uncertainties, lacunae, and even some contradictions in the biographical data that have come down to us. Modern scholarship has served us well in tracing a careful way through the sometimes conflicting claims of the past. Its efforts have delineated an even more faithful portrait of this holy virgin, whom her spiritual daughters lovingly recognize, honor, and follow as their mother and foundress, their "model and mirror."

There is one peculiarity to which we must give attention: the writings about Saint Clare's life that come to us from the thirteenth century are generally referred to as "hagiographical" rather than strictly biographical. This means that the author recorded those personal qualities and events in the life of the Saint which mainly testify to the holiness of the subject; they are intended to edify the reader. This is not to say they are not true, but only that they were selected with a very limited purpose in mind. Also, they inevitably reflected the contemporary model of sanctity which stressed miracles, the unusual, and extraordinary events. So we shall look in vain for many of the very human details which we, in our day, love to recall about those whom we admire.

Yet, as recently as 1920, a valuable document was discovered — the Process of Canonization, which records the interviews conducted on the order of Pope Innocent IV to confirm the universal consensus about the holiness of life of one he did not hesitate to call, even prematurely, "Saint Clare."

Clare died in August of 1253. The interviews were conducted in November of the same year, and the witnesses were all testifying to relatively recent events. Most of those questioned were Sisters of the community of San Damiano, some of whom had lived with Saint Clare from the Order's beginnings. Several had even known her quite well before she left her parental home. Since all testimony was given under solemn oath in the context of ecclesiastical procedure, we are assured of factual reliability. The directness and candor of the recorded testimony colors our picture of Saint Clare in warm, human tones even as it overwhelmingly exalts her reputation for sanctity. This recorded testimony now available in the Process makes clear the fidelity of the ancient, hagiographical "Legend" for which it was the source.

In the present account, the temptation to fill in Saint Clare's story where information is lacking has been avoided. Even so, occasional liberty has been employed to "report" what would be the almost inevitable human response to a situation, even though this may not be historically documented. For example, we may well believe that Clare's mother smiled, as any mother would, to see her little girl counting her prayers with a row of pebbles. Employing such means simply assists the narrative to reflect all the fascination, sparkle, and joy which have not dimmed through the centuries. It even seems to grow in luster and beauty through successive generations of Poor Clare living. Just as with the Gospel of our Lord Jesus Christ, when faithful followers reflect upon what has been recorded, so the richness, depth, and beauty of Clare's story continually unfolds, because this is a living word. This is a *life*!

I rejoice heartily in the LORD,
in my God is the joy of my soul;
For he has clothed me with a robe of salvation,
and wrapped me in a mantle of justice . . .
like a bride bedecked with her jewels.[1]
— Isaiah 61:10

Possibly one of the loveliest words of the Good News we have received by faith in Jesus and his Church is that every one of us is "clothed with a robe of salvation." The Blessed Virgin Mary is the one on whom the liturgy bestows this text from Isaiah in a preeminent way. Following her, and along with her, the saints, whom God calls from our midst, are those in whom this "robe" is tangible, in whom salvation shines, so that they are in truth "clothed in gladness" for all to see and celebrate.

In the galaxy of all the saints, Saint Clare of Assisi stands out as a new star. She was clothed with salvation and gladness like a bride, and her life unfolded within God's favor and his choice of her.

Her story is true, truer than words can express. And it is beautiful. Her rejoicing led her to the carefree and total abandonment of poverty, understood as joyful trust in her Father. She called him "Largitor," a Latin word which nearly defies translation, but literally means "a big spender!" She entrusted her all to his keeping, and entered into a life like Jesus, his Son, who gave himself up for our salvation. Doing this with and in Jesus, Clare discovered with Jesus that her mourning was turned into dancing and the Father took off her sackcloth and clothed her in gladness. Under the influence of the Spirit's action, her beauty was unparalleled, belonging to a celestial order.

Near the end of her life she wrote to a much-loved protégée the secret of her beauty, which we are also privileged to learn. In her letter to Saint Agnes of Prague, Saint Clare calls Jesus "the radiance of eternal light and the mirror without flaw." She urges, "Gaze into that mirror daily . . . so that you may adorn yourself, clothed entirely, inwardly and outwardly, with diverse flowers and garments of all virtues. Indeed this mirror reflects blessed poverty, holy humility, and a charity beyond words, just as, with the grace of God, you can contemplate them."[2] Saint Clare holds up to us the poverty of Our Lord, who was wrapped in swaddling clothes, the labors he endured for us, and, finally, the love that led him to suffer and die on the Cross. In this way she was truly "clothed with a robe of salvation"; and as she came to reflect God more and more by her virtue, she was, as the time of her death, "wrapped in a mantle of justice" — of holiness. And when Our Lord brought her into the bridal chamber of heaven she was eternally "robed in light as with a cloak,"[3] clothed in gladness and covered with a robe of glory.

Saint Clare of Assisi from a 13th-Century Fresco

Valley of the Tescio

Chapter One

Rise up in splendor!
Your light has come.
— Isaiah 60:1

The times and the world into which Saint Clare was born were in many ways like our own. There was greed all about and the economy was shifting; there were power struggles and wars; there was the timeless result of these things which seem to be humanity's consistent contribution in fulfilling at least one of our Lord's promises: "The poor you always have with you."[4]

The wars seemed endless; their protagonists were often as not popes and emperors with factious allegiances feuding all about, rending and splitting all Christendom. The one factor that provided some cohesive force was also military in nature, though noble by proposed purpose: the Crusades. A rebound effect of the expansion the Crusades occasioned was the escalation of commerce and the immense stimulation of imagination and new trends of thought and ideas. This was the turn of events which created new terms for power struggles at home: the rise in wealth of the common people, the artisans, and the merchants, who soon discovered that "money talks" and who wanted to have their say and to be listened to. No longer was noble birth the sole claim to incontestable social privilege. The feudal system was in peril and a new order was forming beneath the surface.

Assisi was a more than typical scene of movement and activity in the sociopolitical sphere of the Italian peninsula. A small but ancient city perched on the slopes of Mount Subasio in the duchy of Spoleto; history's play of light and shadows had passed over this vulnerable yet strategic site and had left its mark on the citizens. It was deeply immersed in the tensions of the times as the twelfth century strode confidently towards its close with the strange mixture of prophecies — now doom, now utopia — that usually herald the turn of a century.

So we of our age recognize the terms and the dynamics, even though the customs, mentalities, and styles of twelfth-century Italy were different. To paraphrase the poet, "men may come and men may go"[5] but human nature goes on forever. Perhaps the men were a little more blustery and the women a little more pious than in our day; the teenagers were rowdy and babies were precious packets of promise.

It was such a precious packet that was borne in high ceremony across the piazza of San Rufino one July day in 1194.[6] The pomp and circumstance swirled about the Offreduccio clan and the cortege moved solemnly through the warm, sun-lit street towards the Cathedral[7] and its baptistry.

Favarone di Offreduccio and his six brothers, including Monaldo and Scipione, were knights of standing, and the noble family was an official protector of Assisi's revered Cathedral of San Rufino. Their palazzo was on the piazza just next to the imposing structure. Favarone's devout wife, Ortulana, had given birth to a daughter. She was a child of promise in more than the usual sense of that expression because, not long before the infant's birth, the mother, anxious about a safe delivery, had prayed before a crucifix in a nearby church for help and protection. She distinctly heard the words, "Do not be afraid, woman, for you will give birth in safety to a light which will give light more clearly than light itself."[8]

So at that moment in the rite of holy Baptism when the child's Christian name is given, this daughter of noble lineage was named Chiara, Clare, the clear and radiant light.

The baptismal font in San Rufino may still be seen today as well as a testimonial commemorating the spot where the first steps of a remarkable spiritual journey were taken by two of Assisi's favored children: Francis and Clare.

And so, marked with the Sign of the Cross, and clothed with the robe of salvation, this small but very clear light began to shine. She was unmistakably endowed by nature, with her golden hair and bright eyes, quick intelligence and winning ways; she was unquestionably the daughter of noble stock, one in a line of proud and courageous soldiers. If Favarone felt any small regret that this child was not a son who would carry on the noble name and tradition of the Offreduccio, he was soon charmed and captivated by his lively and engaging young daughter. In time, she would surely bring luster to the clan through a brilliant marriage alliance.

Clare, however, was even more blessed by grace, and her spiritually-minded mother was diligent and watchful to foster her lovely daughter's strongly Christian disposition. Ortulana was keen to feed the girl's devotional inclinations by instructing her quick mind in the truths of the faith, and the little girl seemed to have a hunger to know about our Lord. Ortulana, who had made the arduous pilgrimage to the Holy Land, imparted her own fervor, telling Clare about the mysteries of Jesus' life and all that she had seen and heard when her own feet had followed the steps he had walked to Calvary. The mother would smile as she watched her daughter, so seriously intent on her prayers, keeping count of her "Our Fathers" by a line, then a pile of little pebbles.

The little Clare had only begun to be quite sure on her feet and to find her way around her expanding world in the family home when a wonderful thing happened: a new baby was born and Clare had tiny Catherine as a treasured sister. Other than Beatrice, another sister, we know nothing more of the family circle. In years to come, Clare's biographer would hail her as "a brilliant light for women . . . a new leader of women."[9] Possibly it was because she had received a good apprenticeship very early in life. Her sisters — and even her mother — must have looked to this child of predilection with something akin to awe.

Life in a medieval household for people of station was somewhat ritualized but not necessarily predictable.

Rocca Maggiore

When Clare was about four years old, the growing rest-lessness of the "minores," the upcoming social party in Assisi, erupted into violence provoked by political events among the nobility, which the citizens interpreted as clearly treasonous. Taking advantage of the absence of Duke Conrad, their despised foreign overlord, the common Assisians stormed the fortress castle of Rocca Maggiore and began tearing it down. (With more circumspection than one normally finds in mobs, they saved the stones to build up the city walls. Apparently they intuitively sensed they would need strong city walls.) Then, with the indiscriminateness typical of mobs, they turned upon the palaces of all the nobility. The members of the Offreduccio household had to flee for their lives, becoming exiles for several years in Perugia. That the nobility, generally, sought haven under the protection of Assisi's ancient archenemy, Perugia, poured fuel on the fires of reckless wrath burning in the hearts of the "minores." The fact that these nobles had little alternative seemed lost on the powers-that-now-be.

Clare's family took up life in the neighboring commune of Perugia with some semblance of security, and the child's education and spiritual growth continued under the watchful eye and skilled hand of Lady Ortulana. The radiance of this young daughter of Favarone and her profound goodness, mature beyond her age, was noted by the families of Perugia among whom she lived during this period of banishment. Strong ties of friendship were forged which would bear fruit in later years.

In 1205, the situation in Assisi normalized, and a peace of sorts was patched up while the local nobles quietly filtered back into civic life. Clare was again bringing luster to her native soil. Contemporary accounts consistently trace this light to a more than natural source. "...The Spirit inflaming and molding her interiorly, she became known as a most pure vessel, a vessel of graces."[10]

She was growing in that strong yet tender compassion for the poor and suffering which would always characterize her life. Nor did Lady Ortulana curb the missions of mercy undertaken by the young Clare, who eagerly made personal sacrifices to aid the poor and needy. She deprived herself of delicate foods and sent them secretly to the poor.[11]

Such goodness, added to charm and intelligence, totaled to outstanding beauty, not missed by those who were seeking a fortunate marriage. But these same qualities equipped the young Clare with an astuteness in excess of her betters. She sidestepped the prospect of marriage skillfully and repeatedly. And her life of devotion and reflection matured into a prayer that was a deep relationship. She knew him in whom she had believed. Her desire to be with the Lord and to be united to him was surpassed by only one thing: his desire for her.

The goal was clear with the clarity that gave this young light her name. But the path to the goal was obscure.

From a 13th-Century Painting of Saint Clare

Chapter Two

... Called by a new name.
— Isaiah 62:2

Another young citizen of Assisi had stood uncertain at the crossroads of life just a few years earlier. His name was Francis. He had abandoned himself to the "games" of wealth, power, and adventure. But then a series of events brought him face to face with the meaning of life and the destiny of his immortal spirit. Francis encountered God. With the spontaneous, wholehearted investment of himself typical of this generous youth, Francis followed Christ unreservedly. The same colorful imagination which had made him a debonair man about town now lent an air of romance to his religious dedication.

How Clare first heard of Francis or at what point she began to take him seriously or feel personally attracted by his gospel life of poverty is not known. More than a decade her senior and the son of a common, though wealthy and influential cloth merchant, Francesco di Pietro di Bernadone had emerged as a total surprise. Francis gave Assisi that something stunningly "new" which people are always predicting but never really expect. His about-face conversion from one set of eccentric ways to another set of even more eccentric ways was well-known throughout the area. There had been among Assisi's citizens a subtle attitudinal shift from jeering skepticism toward a realization that this was "for real," which left many in puzzlement and some in admiration. A few even followed suit! And not the bumpkins, either.

First came Bernardo di Quintavalle, a much-respected citizen. Not long after, the casualties struck the Offreduccio household, and Clare's cousin Rufino, son of her uncle Scipione, went to join the Little Poor Man.

Apparently Francis took the initiative with Clare. If he was well-known in town by his sensational reversal, Clare was equally, though less controversially, the subject of conversation and speculation in Assisi's circles. As her early biographer poetically reports:

As
a chest of so many perfumes,
even though closed,
reveals its contents by its fragrance;
so
she unknowingly began to be praised
and,
when true recognition of her secret deeds appeared,
the account of her goodness
was spread among the people.[12]

When Francis had first begun his strange mission and manner of life, he had set about restoring tumbled-down chapels in Assisi's environs, beginning with San Damiano, where in prayer he had been told by a voice from the crucifix there, "Go, repair my house."[13] Many years later Clare would relate in her spiritual Testament, joining her testimony to other chroniclers, that Francis was one day seized by the Holy Spirit in prophecy and, mounting the walls of San Damiano, called out in French to poor people nearby, "Come and help me in the work of the monastery of San Damiano, for in that place later on will be ladies by whose renowned and holy way of living our heavenly Father will be glorified throughout all his holy Church."[14] What more was possibly revealed to him at that moment is not known, but it is highly unlikely that he would have forgotten this singular experience, or would not have seen it as somehow deeply intertwined with his own call.

There are some souls in whom sanctity is almost tangible, and the purity of holiness virtually radiates from their countenances. One may safely assume that Clare was such a soul because several witnesses in the process for her canonization testified that she was unimaginably holy, so much so that they could compare her to no one other than the Blessed Virgin Mary.[15] When Francis heard of her fame and saw her with his own eyes, most likely the Spirit cause him to recognize: this is she!

And so the ancient biographer relates, "[Francis] visited her and she more frequently him. . . . The Father Francis encouraged her to despise the world, showing her by his living speech how dry the hope of the world was and how deceptive its beauty. He whispered in her ears of a sweet espousal with Christ, persuading her to preserve the pearl of her virginal purity for that blessed Spouse Whom Love made man."[16]

Thus began one of the most celebrated relationships in history. There has been too much speculation about this relationship, with poetic imagination rashly attempting to glamorize a profoundly sacred reality. It is understandable. One would nearly have to be caught up in the spiritual orbit in which these two saints moved to be able to comment on a relationship at one and the same time so radically human and yet so angelically spiritual. If we cannot enter into such depths of holiness where God is all in all, at least we may base our appreciation of this blessed friendship on the clear testimony of contemporary witnesses and then praise God, who has given some of his children such gifts of spiritual sublimity along with such human warmth.

Clare's heart was soon entirely captivated. The path she was to take in giving herself to God alone was finally clear. She recalls it in simple words toward the end of her life with the same freshness and enthusiasm that possessed her heart in the early spring of 1212: "The Son of God became for us the way which our blessed Father Francis, his true ardent lover and imitator, has shown and taught us by word and example."[17]

There is a spontaneity about the early Franciscan movement which would almost suggest a haphazard recklessness. When we read between the lines, however, we especially note an evident care to proceed along new ways with the blessing of the Church. And for Francis and Clare (and all Assisi at that time) the Church was personified in His Lordship, Guido, Bishop of Assisi. Whatever else may be true of this shepherd, he did possess the spiritual insight to recognize very early the finger of God in the unusual call of Francis of Assisi at a time when others had only suspicion and contempt for it. Guido also had the courage of his convictions and at least quietly supported the new movement, and seems even to have offered fatherly guidance and protection. There is reason to believe that Bishop Guido knew and approved of the plan of Chiara di Favarone di Offreduccio to leave her parental home and follow Christ in the gospel poverty of Francis and his "lesser brothers," thus entering a religious Order which did not yet exist — at least not for women. Bishop Guido was probably not used to playing supporting roles, but on Palm Sunday of 1212, he took deep pleasure in his small part in one of the most stirring dramas of history.

Street in Assisi

Chapter Three

Like a bride bedecked with her jewels.
— Isaiah 61:10

Color, pageantry, and imagery combine to make the story of Clare's espousal to Christ one of the most attractive pages in the lives of the saints. Medieval social life was closely linked to the Church in her festivals. Thus on Palm Sunday, the solemn entry of our Lord Jesus Christ into Jerusalem was ritually re-enacted with an enthusiastic demonstration of triumph and joy. All Assisi turned out garbed in finery for the blessing of palms and a procession of splendor, color, and song. The young Lady Clare seemed to have taken exceptional care to enhance her striking beauty with jeweled adornment and rich brocades which set off her fair complexion and golden hair and created a stunning picture. Her charm was augmented by a graceful modesty that revealed the unearthly beauty of a splendor shining forth from the clear light within her. Undoubtedly, heads turned as this daughter of the Offreduccio, accompanied by the household's knights and the other ladies no less magnificently attired, made their impressive way through the piazza to the Cathedral.

The eighteen-year-old Clare took her place and the solemn liturgical service began. If Clare's beauty was singular among the other young women, her devotion and piety made her even more prominent as she became totally absorbed in the sacred rites which held so deep a symbolism for her. No one, except possibly the pontifical celebrant Bishop Guido, could have guessed the ardent thoughts which swelled her soul and overflowed into her senses, transfixing her in a world of the spirit, accessible only to one of deep prayer. The bridal adornment of her dress was only a faint image of the bridal love that possessed her heart. She was deeply in touch with the sacred mysteries being celebrated that day and she saw far beyond the moment of "Hosannas" and the flush of waving palms. Jesus was entering into his hour, his redemptive suffering and death. Like his true bride, Clare was prepared to follow him into the heart of the paschal mystery. Later her biographer would cite the Letter to the Hebrews and say that since Jesus suffered outside the gate, she would go to him outside the camp and share his degradation.[18]

The other young ladies were filing forward to receive their palm branches from the Bishop, but Clare, occupied with her reflections, stayed quietly in her place. A stir went through the assembly as something wholly unprecedented took place. Bishop Guido, quite aware of the noble and fervent bride who had held back, left his place in the sanctuary and came directly to Clare, offering her the palm so sacred with symbolism. For an instant she surely must have evoked the popular stories of the young virgin martyrs of old. And possibly this was not far from the actual fact. Clare was to take the palm and go forth courageously to give her very life in faith and love for Christ.

The Bishop returned to his place and resumed the service as if his unusual gesture had been just a part of the ceremonial.

Festivities extended throughout the day in the Offreduccio household, as did the deep recollection that accompanied the brave resolve of its favored daughter.

Dusk fell and, little by little, the house settled down for the night like a great roosting bird to its sleep. Only one was watchful: Clare. When all was silent, still dressed in her bridal finery she stirred from her room, quietly slipping through the dark corridors her feet knew so well, without needing light to see. Avoiding the main door with its sentry guard, she made her way to the secondary door, locked, boarded, and even barricaded with large stones. Sister Christiana testified many years later that this door "could not be opened even by a large number of men. [Clare] alone, with the help of Jesus Christ, removed [the stones] and opened the door. On the following morning, when many people saw that door opened, they were somewhat astonished at how a young girl could have done it."[19]

Clare had always taken care that her clandestine meetings with Francis be duly chaperoned. Bona, the daughter of Guelfuccio of Assisi, who usually accompanied her, was spending Lent in Rome. On this occasion another figure, whose mysterious identity remains unknown, glided from the shadows to the side of this bride, brilliantly sparkling in the night as the moonlight glanced off her jeweled finery. Together they cautiously made their way through a gate in the city wall, past a blinded, bribed, or bedazzled sentry and into the dark forest towards the chapel of Our Lady of Angels, also called Saint Mary of the Portiuncula, where Francis and his "knights" held high court before the throne of the Mother of God.

The two figures sped through the night with only the skies and their thousand stars as witnesses. Possibly Clare remembered this flight years later when she wrote to the Bohemian princess Agnes of Prague, who had become her spiritual daughter, "With swift pace, light step, unstumbling feet, so that your movement does not even stir up the dust, may you cautiously climb upwards, serene, joyful, and eager, on the way of blessedness."[20]

Then, at some distance, flecks of light darted through the dense trees like fireflies on a summer night. Clare knew it was Francis and the Brothers with torches, coming, as had been arranged, to meet and escort her to the Portiuncula. Heaven alone has recorded the instant of meeting, when Francis's whole soul shook with divine presentiment that a moment had begun which would mysteriously reach into eternity and would have no end. With exquisite courtesy and courtly bearing, the Little Poor Man led this Princess of Poverty to her tryst with God Most High.

In the little church of Saint Mary of the Portiuncula, which for all time will be reverenced as the cradle of both the Order of the Friars Minor and that of the Poor Ladies, unfolded a simple ceremony. Brother Francis cut the golden halo of Clare's lovely hair. The Brothers brought forward the "habit of penance," undoubtedly assembled in the finest tradition of needlework! But to Clare it was the image of all she desired, and with deliberate swiftness she exchanged for it her costly jewels and gown, which she cast aside. Did anyone present at that moment realize the totally new and even revolutionary nature of what had just been done? If its reality had up to this point eluded them, the coming days' events would bring home the magnitude of the act.

From a 13th-Century Painting of Saint Clare

Chapter Four

You shall know that I, the LORD, am your savior.
— Isaiah 60:16

Having virtually received Clare into the Brotherhood, Francis left with her immediately, accompanied by their companions, and took her to the Benedictine monastery of San Paolo delle Abbadesse in nearby Bastia. This was apparently according to a well-planned strategy. No one was naïve enough to think Clare's disappearance would pass without comment in the Offreduccio household! On the other hand, the good nuns of San Paolo had evidently underestimated the uproar that would soon throw their Holy Week observance of the most solemn liturgies of the Church year into a bedlam of violence and confusion.

But briefly, for perhaps the first few days of Holy Week, life was quite regular. While Clare was an exceedingly graced person, intelligent, generous, and spiritually mature beyond her years, she still needed the experience of living religious life in a well-ordered, monastic setting. So like thousands of postulants before and after her, Clare learned the manner of praying the choral Divine Office and applied herself to conforming to monastic mores and usages. Perhaps she was bewildered, as most postulants are, by the intricacies of schedules, processions, and customs, which all the other nuns seem to have mastered as effortlessly as second nature. Probably, because of her delicate sensitivity to all things beautiful, she was swifter than the average newcomer to note the exquisite courtesy and sisterly charity embodied within the liturgical ceremonies and the monastic code of daily living.

Soon enough came the anticipated signs: the commotion at the monastery gate; the formidable group of knightly relatives with a thin veneer of respectability, asking, demanding, to see her; the kind words and promises which quickly degenerated into threats, then curses, then violence. What these noble knights had failed to calculate was the effect of their own brave blood flowing in the veins of this noble lady of their stock. And she had now espoused a cause and a Lord "of more noble lineage, whose power is stronger, excellence more lofty, whose countenance more beautiful, love sweeter, and whose every courtesy more exquisite . . . who for the sake of us all bore the suffering of the Cross."[21] So the young girl stood firm "in the holy service [she] had just begun out of a burning desire for the poor Crucified."[22] With sure instinct, swift decision, and a strength beyond her own, she sped — was, in fact, nearly borne by the Holy Spirit acting in her — to the monastic church. There she clung to the altar cloth, a gesture which assured her the sacrosanct protection of sanctuary. The message was not lost on the relatives who had followed in hot pursuit. With their fury so far beyond the control of reason, there was danger they would not even respect that inviolable institution of sanctuary and would allow their rage to lead them off the brink into excommunication and all its attendant consequences. Clare, assessing the crisis of that moment, pulled away the veil of consecration she wore, thus exposing her tonsured head to the view of these "brave and gallant" knights. It had the desired effect. They were stunned into confusion; their spiraling momentum was countered by the force of the incomprehensible, like the glance of Yahweh which cast confusion into the ranks of the enemy.[23] They slipped away, vanquished.

In order to understand the magnitude and violence of the family reaction, it is necessary to enter into the mentality of medieval feudal family structure with its code of honor, dependence on loyalty, and the upholding of a value system which was warp and woof of its fabric. This was the law of the clan, and what Clare had done was a "criminal act" and, worse still, an affront. The noble knights were haughty and proud. There was one thing no one was allowed to do: publicly humiliate them. Clare's desertion was perceived as just that, a flagrant humiliation. In the world of the Middle Ages there were two ways of resolving disputes: the law courts and brute force. The knightly class spent most of its time between these two "noble" activities. Law courts were, of course, time-consuming and tedious. In this instance legal procedures were completely inadequate.

The Benedictine community of nuns of San Paolo was not without its legal fortification and well-defined powers. Papal privileges with sanctions of excommunication protected their rights against such intrusions and threats to peace and property. But Clare, as a guest to whom hospitality had been graciously extended, was in no sense protected by such legal coverage. And the Offreduccio household was powerful, its knights strong and angry. Wishing her well, the nuns of San Paolo suggested she find another home.

So Francis came with Bernard and Philip and took Clare to the safety of San Angelo in Panzo, some distance away on the eastern slope of Monte Subasio. Situated again within a community, Clare found herself still alone for want of companions with whom she could share fully her spiritual aspirations and idealism. She began to pray to our Lord for the grace of conversion for her beloved sister Catherine, younger by two years. The biographer recounts, "The divine majesty answered without delay . . . and quickly gave her that first gift that she so eagerly sought and that was so greatly pleasing to God to present."[24] Only sixteen days after Clare's flight from the family home, Catherine also fled to her sister's side to join Clare in the service of God.

The story continues, "While the joyous sisters were clinging to the footprints of Christ in the church of San Angelo in Panzo and she who had heard more from the Lord was teaching her novice-sister, new attacks by relatives were quickly flaring up against the young girls."[25] Twelve men, led by Uncle Monaldo, seemed civil enough at first and asked Catherine to return with them. She refused. Then they ordered her to return. Again she refused, saying that she did not want to leave her sister Clare. The ancient writer's comment at this point is telling when he reports, "They had long ago lost hope of Clare!"[26]

Having exhausted their store of logic, the men resorted to force and, with kicks and blows, began to carry, drag, and pull the young girl with them. She resisted with all her strength, and the violence escalated until the path was strewn with bits of Catherine's hair and clothing. She cried out in her distress to Clare, "Dear sister, help me! Do not let me be taken from Christ the Lord!"[27] And the first record is left to us of God's miraculous intervention in response to the prayer of the holy virgin Clare.

Catherine's body suddenly became so heavy that her would-be captors were powerless to lift her. Farmhands, running in from the fields to help, were likewise unable to move the frail form from the spot where she had fallen. In a crude jest, the men shrugged off the obvious providential occurrence saying, "She has been eating lead all night; no wonder she is so heavy!"[28] But the Lord Monaldo did not think the situation at all humorous. He raised his strong arm, intending to strike his own niece a lethal blow, when piercing pain and paralysis afflicted him on the spot and brought the whole incident to an impasse. At this point Clare approached the dazed group with her simple solution: they should all go home and leave Catherine, "half dead on the ground,"[29] to her. The proud knights brushed off their dignity and left "with a bitter spirit at their unfinished business."[30] The two sisters returned to San Angelo, rejoicing not only over their victory, but also over their good fortune at having been found worthy to suffer for the Cross of Christ.

It was after this trial that Francis received Catherine into the Order, cutting her hair himself and giving her the name Sister Agnes in honor of the youthful virgin martyr of the early Church. This very young girl had given evidence of valor comparable to her holy patroness.

While there was great happiness for the two sisters in their shared life and ideals, there was also a restlessness. San Angelo had given them the sense of regularity and ordered life of a religious institution, but it was far from the expression of poverty, prayer, and community to which they were irresistibly drawn by the inspiration of Francis and his Brothers. So the day came when Brother Francis arrived at San Angelo with glad tidings for Clare and Agnes: San Damiano was ready for them!

Detail of San Damiano Crucifix

Chapter Five

They shall rebuild the ancient ruins.
— Isaiah 61:4

San Damiano. The very sound of the name evokes in the Franciscan heart an awe, a spirit of joy and repose. San Damiano is a synonym for peace, for poverty, for contemplation and the constancy of one woman's devotion. "In this little house of penance the virgin Clare enclosed herself for love of her heavenly spouse."[31]

It was springtime in Umbria. The new wheat was glistening in the furrows, the sap was rising in the trees where tender blossoms were unfolding, the rushes were alive with bristling activity, the sky was intensely blue, and the whole slope of ancient Monte Subasio seemed young and new again. Nature found echo in the spirits of a poor band of joyous pilgrims. Francis led Clare and Agnes down the lane flanked with budding olive trees to their new home. He took them inside and showed them the very poor, bare rooms which he presented to them as their "monastery." It would do quite well. More than that. It was perfect! It was positively glorious: the earthly dwelling place of Christ's dear bride, Lady Poverty.

Then they came into the presence of that Crucified Love who had spoken to Francis. Clare gazed into those two great eyes of the painted crucifix that pierced her soul with a look of most profound love. Jesus would be her "vow" of stability as she took her stand with Mary, the *Stabat Mater*, beneath the Cross. He was the place's only adornment. And it was enough.

47

No details are left to posterity about the first days when, together, those two young girls began to draw the outlines for monastic living. The deep respect Clare was to manifest for her Sisters throughout her life would seem to guarantee that Agnes would have had a large part in the practical arranging of community life, and apparently Francis kept rather close contact during those early days and weeks. Both Francis and Clare would later direct their followers to desire, above all human endeavor, "To have the Spirit of the Lord and his holy way of working."[32] These are not mere words, but a program of life. And when the Holy Spirit finds this kind of liberty in souls, his manner of working is truly marvelous.

The light of Clare, placed, as it were, like a vigil light before the Crucifix of San Damiano, began not only to

San Damiano

radiate but to send forth living sparks which very soon enkindled other hearts. Clare and Agnes were joined by Pacifica di Guelfuccio, an older lady of the nobility who had been very close to Clare and to her mother Ortolana, having accompanied the latter on her pilgrimages, including the one to the Holy Land.

It was springtime in Umbria. And the names of the Poor Ladies who followed in the train of the Princess of Poverty sound like the song of the early winds filtering through the silvery olive trees: Pacifica, Benvenuta, Philippa, Gineva who became Benedetta, Christiana, Balvina, Francesca, and more. Clare's biographer was to describe it this way: "In the hollow of this wall, the silver-winged dove, building a nest, gave birth to a gathering of virgins of Christ, founded a holy monastery, and began the Order of the Poor Ladies."[33] Yes, it was springtime in Umbria.

Francis was stirred. He felt his own spiritual vision swept into the brightness and beauty of this barefoot Sister who somehow brought a freshness to it, something indefinable but very truly new. Hers was a spiritual genius, wholly unassuming and totally unself-conscious, and so all the more pure, limpid, and powerful. Francis found a sense of peace in his sureness that the gospel life of poverty would always be revered and fully lived here in San Damiano, come what may.

Many years later Clare would recall, "I, together with the few Sisters whom the Lord had given me a little while after my conversion, freely promised [Francis] obedience as the Lord bestowed on us the light of his grace through that praiseworthy life and teaching."[34]

As Francis and his Brothers observed Clare and her

poor little community at San Damiano, he probably recalled those idyllic days with the Brothers at Rivo Torto. Their poverty had been extreme but so had been their mutual love and their abandonment to the Lord in the freedom of prayer. The fruits of the Spirit were tangible for them all in a unique way: charity, joy, peace, patience, kindness. Now the Sisters were caught up in the simplicity of their own pure beginnings. Francis could scarcely have hoped for more ardent disciples than these Poor Ladies of San Damiano, and he poured out the full enthusiasm of his burning spirit into their eager hearts, urging them along Christ's way of poverty and humility. As for his Friars at Rivo Torto, so now for the Sisters, Francis added to his teaching and example a simple "form of life." Clare would later incorporate these words into her Rule saying:

> And observing, indeed, that we did not fear any poverty, labor, trial, scorn and contempt of the world, but rather that we held them as great delights, the blessed Father, moved by compassion, wrote for us a form of life as follows: "Since by divine inspiration you have made yourselves daughters and handmaids of the most high sovereign King, the heavenly Father, and have espoused yourselves to the Holy Spirit by choosing to live according to the perfection of the holy Gospel, I will and I promise for myself and my Brothers always to have for you, even as for them, loving care and special solicitude."[35]

To live according to the perfection of the Gospel was, then, the ideal Francis set before them, and so Sacred

Scripture became the daily bread of Clare and her Sisters. They prayed, reflected on, and lived by the Word of God. The Gospel according to Saint Matthew was apparently a favorite one for both Francis and Clare, possibly because of the radicality of its message, the swift response to the call of the Master, and the loving reliance on the Father's providence related in those pages. The Sermon on the Mount is sometimes described as a primer for the spiritual life. It is not difficult to discover in Matthew's account an apt picture of the spiritual program for the Sisters of San Damiano. Under the tutelage of their gifted teacher, they very quickly reaped the fruits of blessed happiness promised in the Beatitudes to the poor in spirit, the meek, the merciful, the pure of heart, and those who suffer persecution for the sake of holiness. Clare, in her Rule, cites this last Beatitude,[36] and one wonders how long the "Magnificent City of Assisi" held out against the indignity of its loveliest daughters slipping out its southeasterly gates to join Clare at San Damiano.

The rhythm of monastic life is interwoven with the Church's sacred liturgy. Both rise and fall gently with the succession of feasts and fasts, seasons and observances in a kind of timelessness, or rather a transcendence of the ordinary historical measures of time. The Sisters gave themselves to the choral recitation of the Divine Office by day and by night. All of daily life was arranged about this holy and unifying prayer which nourished their spirits and made of their lives a great hymn of praise. The prayer of the Church and the prayer of their hearts became an atmosphere in which Clare and the Poor Ladies generously gave themselves to the Lord for his Church and for souls.

All the essentials of religious life were falling into place as the community increased; all, that is, but one. Francis began to urge upon Clare that she assume the office and role of abbess among her Sisters. There was probably a certain tilt of her head, a lift of the chin, and a white flash in her eye when this daughter of the Offreduccio took a strong stand. Later on popes would note it and accord it a certain respect, not to say awe. Clare clung to her lowly estate as a poor virgin among her poor Sisters more tenaciously than those jealous for power jockeyed for worldly positions. Possibly, Bishop Guido had to be called in to support the case; possibly, it was Francis' own gospel view of authority as humble service; possibly, as Pacifica suggests in her testimony in the Process of Canonization many years later, Francis "almost forced her."[37] Whatever the means, Clare did finally accept the title and the office of Abbess of the Poor Ladies of San Damiano. In doing so, she recast the traditional position of prestige and social privilege into a new model of a delicately balanced, spirit-filled leadership, which would challenge the fervor and fidelity of all the Sisters by loving example and encouragement. The abbess would be, as she would describe it, "the handmaid of all the Sisters."[38] Clare was to be Mother as well as Sister.

Santa Chiara

Chapter Six

As the earth brings forth its plants . . . so will the Lord
God make justice spring up before all the nations.
— Isaiah 61:11

Being Abbess and Mother of her community at San
Damiano carried no privileges or honorary exceptions attached to the office; quite the contrary. If Clare was to
ask her Sisters to be models and mirrors to one another,
even more would her responsibilities place this sacred
charge upon her. She spent long hours of the day and
night in prayer and contemplation, intensely absorbed
in the love of her Crucified Lord. It was as if she inces-
santly heard the cry of Little Brother Francis, "I weep for
the passion of my Lord Jesus Christ."[39] These words were
like a dart of wounded love penetrating her heart, and
she would respond with all the ardor of her own spirit in
compassion and devotion.

Words were not enough; sighs were not enough; tears
were not enough. From her youth Clare's love had found
expression, almost relief, in fasting and works of penance. The more she experienced the release of her power
to love through these practices, the more did she multi-
ply them. In fact, she multiplied them to the point of
imprudence. She began to fast totally from food on Monday, Wednesday, and Friday. In spite of her glowing cheer-
fulness and affability with her daughters, they began to
be alarmed at the extreme hardship Clare was placing on
her body. Sister Pacifica later reports in her testimony
for the Process of Canonization that Clare "developed a

certain illness"[40] because of her extreme fasting. Pacifica confessed that she herself had often wept over the situation. It seems their Mother Clare was heedless of their entreaties. The Sisters had only one other recourse.

So it was that the young Abbess was summoned to the parlor one day. There her luminous and smiling face was greeted by a solemn Brother Francis and an even more solemn Bishop Guido. Apparently these two sought the fortification of each other's influence whenever it was matter of presenting to the Holy Mother of the Poor Ladies a proposition which she was surely not to favor. "Every day. *Every single day!*"[41] Clare was not to let a single day pass without eating at least one half a bun! Amen. Whether or not the other Sisters of San Damiano were very consoled by this, the two churchmen left the monastery feeling victorious. And the holy Mother, who valued obedience far above any work of mortification, brought her offering before the Lord and was faithful for the many years to come to the limits Francis placed on her.

Obviously the adjustments were inadequate; the harm was already done to the constitution of one basically strong but delicately reared. There were many contributing factors, and the health of Clare was undermined — indeed, it was broken. The precise nature of her illnesses is unknown; but serious illness was her portion for twenty-eight years, beginning shortly before the death of Saint Francis and continuing until her own death in 1253.

Clare would write to Agnes of Prague around the year 1238 that "our flesh is not a flesh of bronze nor our strength the strength of stone. Rather, we are frail and subject to every bodily weakness. I have learned that you have set about a certain different and impossible austerity in fasting, and I ask you, dearest one, to be wisely and sensibly restrained."[42] What she did not tell her sister-abbess was that she had learned this wisdom by her own difficult experience.

Francis, and even more especially the holy Mother Clare, watched over the Sisters whom the Lord continued to give them. A word often used in the ancient writing describing their concern for the community is "compassion."[43] The poverty was extreme and hardship was the daily lot of the Sisters. Even though they embraced it with such love, joy, and freedom of spirit, their suffering drew forth an active response from their poor little Mother. She prized poverty as their only possession: the mutual treasure of the Poor Christ and his poor virgins. Clare grew daily in her sensitive compassion. Gazing on that great painted figure of the Crucified, meditating on his passion, feeling in her own body the effects of pain and privation, she came to a new realization that it was her compassionate mission in the Church to be "the supporter of the falling members of [Christ's] ineffable Body."[44] Clare passed easily from her profound prayer to acts of loving compassion. Or perhaps it is more correct to say that she never left her prayer, but that it overflowed into her deeds of tender mercy: delicate courtesies like going about silently at night among the sleeping Sisters to make sure they were warmly covered; humble services like washing the feet of the Sisters who served outside the monastery; and then, with the same simple grace, miraculously healing the sick with the sign of the Cross. The Sisters report all these things in the Process of Canonization with candor and admiration, convinced that their much-loved Mother was a Saint.

As Clare's reputation spread so did the charisma and vocation which had been committed to her by the Holy

Spirit. Monasteries were founded, and already existing communities of various traditions, including Benedictine nuns, embraced the life of "most high poverty" as the Damianites lived it. Because the Fourth Lateran Council in 1215 decided to permit no new religious Rules, Clare was formally obliged to accept a Rule based on that of Saint Benedict. From the beginning she had looked to Father Francis, his example and counsels, as her way of life; the Sisters likewise turned to the light of their blessed Mother Clare. The Gospel was enough for them. But the element that was foundational to her, as it was to Francis, was poverty. Because the Sisters were cloistered, their intention to live without possessions, without any stable form of income, and without the freedom to go about begging seemed to many to be a presumptuous, imprudent, and unrealistic ideal. Knowing this, the holy Abbess sought and obtained from Pope Innocent III the Privilege of Poverty in 1216. The Holy See was frequently petitioned for various and sundry privileges, but this was unique among them all! In effect it gave the Poor Ladies permission to live as a community without any property or securities. Such an arrangement was unheard of within the institution of monasticism, particularly for women. The document guaranteed: "no one can compel you to receive possessions."[45] As the *Legend of Saint Clare* records, "The pope himself with great joy wrote with his own hand the first draft of the privilege sought after, so that an unusual favor might smile upon an unusual request."[46] With this, Clare was content. Now and again well-meaning popes and other prelates would, in their deep solicitude and concern for the Poor Ladies, try to urge Clare and her Sisters to accept some form of earthly securities. They went so far as to offer handsome benefices. Possibly Pope Gregory IX, who had long been associated with Francis and Clare as Hugolino, Cardinal Protector of their two Orders, thought he had the solution to the problem when he offered to absolve Clare from her vow of poverty. For the holy Mother there was no problem. Her vow bound her in holy love to the Poor Christ. She replied to his Vicar, "Holy Father, I will never in any way wish to be absolved from the following of Christ."[47] No more words are recorded on the subject, but history makes one further entry on its pages: on September 17, 1228, Gregory IX renewed the Privilege of Poverty.

Clare loved to refer to herself as "the little plant of Saint Francis," who had been her guide and inspiration from the beginning. So vital was his role of "gardener" and so heavily did she count on his promise for his Friars to carry along his same care and solicitude, that Clare regarded this, along with poverty, as essential for her community. Francis had appointed Friars for the spiritual care of the Sisters as well as two Brothers to assist in their temporal needs. As with poverty, this pillar of their relationship to the Friars Minor was tested and at times threatened.

Francis recognized in Clare all the qualities of strength, wisdom, and humility he desired in one whom the Lord called and placed at the head of the Order of Poor Ladies to lead, guide, and form its members. Little by little he withdrew his own direct influence, frequently taking long absences for solitary prayer and journeys in the service of the Gospel. He even traveled to distant Spain, Egypt, and finally the Holy Land, leaving the Poor Ladies, as he did his own Brothers, to the care of the Lord and those who took Francis' place at home. Various circumstances brought the Holy See to a point of interpreting very strictly a counsel in Saint Francis's Rule of 1223. Consequently the pope issued a bull forbidding any Friars to go to the monasteries of the nuns except those to whom special permission was granted by the Holy Father himself. Unfortunately for Clare's good friend, Pope Gregory IX once more found his ingenuity poorly matched. He so distressed the holy Abbess by severely restricting the freedom of the Friars to go to the spiritual assistance of the Poor Ladies, that she summarily dismissed the Brothers who were attached to San Damiano to assist the Sisters in their material needs. She sent them back to the general minister with the lament, "Let him (the pope) now take away from us all the Brothers since he has taken away those who provide us with the [spiritual] food that is vital."[48] Of course, news of this action reached Pope Gregory. Once again history tactfully concludes the story: "He immediately mitigated that prohibition into the hands of the general minister,"[49] in effect returning the care of the Sisters to the successor of Saint Francis.

Well of San Damiano

Chapter Seven

In my God is the joy of my soul.
— Isaiah 61:10

While the calm rhythm of the liturgical seasons passed swiftly like lights and shadows over the months and years of Clare and her daughters, life was in no way uneventful. The Sisters followed closely and supported with prayer and penance the labors of Francis. He had conceived a desire, unheard of in his time, to convert the Muslims. He sent Friar Berard with four companions to Morocco in the spring of 1219, and went himself to the East that autumn. Francis returned, but the others did not. They captured the trophy of martyrdom, further stirring apostolic zeal within the Order and even beyond, drawing new followers such as the Portuguese Augustinian Canon who was to become Saint Anthony of Padua.

Clare herself was fired by a desire to follow the Brothers in this evangelizing effort.[50] Like the young Saint Thérèse of Lisieux, closer to our own times, Clare's "calling" came from the ardor of her spirit, so passionately in love with Christ that she would have wanted to pour out her very substance into every possible vocation and live many lifetimes so as to satisfy her compelling need to give herself ever more completely to him. As Francis was to find his personal martyrdom in a mode other than that of the honored protomartyrs of the Order, so Clare would one day also encounter her Muslims, the Saracens, with a courage equal to her trusting love, without ever leaving her cloister.

Meanwhile, Clare saw and suffered from the disappointment sustained by Saint Francis as the rapid growth of the Brotherhood and the influence of less highly motivated and idealistic members began eroding the early fervor and utter dedication of his first companions. Then Francis resigned as head of the Order. For herself, the holy Abbess did all in her power to support Francis and the other Brothers. At the same time, she took every means to strengthen the bonds of her holy vocation and that of her Sisters by her vital instruction and exhortation, "reflecting," as she would later say, "on the frailty of some others which we kept on fearing in ourselves."[51]

Following his missionary journey to the Holy Land, there was in Francis a great upsurge of devotion to the Incarnation and the Passion of our Lord Jesus Christ. His impressionable soul was fired by the profound experience of walking the very ground his Savior had trod: Bethlehem, Jordan, Jerusalem, Calvary. The penetrating eye of his spirit saw the Lord, and the fire of his heart drove him on to set the world's coldness ablaze. A rich outgrowth of his focus on the Incarnation was a nearly overwhelming realization of the Gift of God in the Holy Eucharist.

Francis realized, as if in a new way, that the life of Jesus was not over. It did not begin and end in the Holy Land. Through the Sacrament of the Altar he was as truly present, and in a sense more truly present, than he had been in Palestine. "O sublime humility! O humble sublimity! That the Lord of the universe, God and the Son of God, so humbles himself that for our salvation he hides himself under the little form of bread!"[52] Clare was so much one spirit with the Poverello that she inhaled his fragrant words and breathed them forth again to her own

Sisters, having brought to them the depth of her own prayer, adoration, and womanly devotion.

Christmas at Greccio in 1223 drew together so many rich and colored threads of the tapestry Francis had been weaving of prayer, preaching, and songs of praise. There the Midnight Mass was celebrated, according to his directions, in high solemnity and with a representation of the Nativity scene of Bethlehem, so that the people could actually see how Love Incarnate came among us and then could in reality receive him in the Holy Eucharist. Saint Francis, deacon at the Solemn High Mass, sang the Gospel of Christmas and preached in a most moving way to the crowds gathered there. Was it for this occasion that Saint Clare made for him the linen alb that is still treasured by her community in Assisi? This precious creation testifies to at least two things: her superb mastery in the tradition of delicate needlework and fashioning of fine Assisi lace and her exalted concept of the stature of Saint Francis. The alb of Saint Francis could have amply housed the Little Poor Man twice over! Possibly she was imbued with the poetic vision of ancient artists who, disregarding realistic proportions, painted very large anyone they considered important. By these standards, Francis emerges as Clare would later describe him, "Our pillar and after God our solitary consolation and strength."[53]

The blessed Father Francis seemed to have about himself a new sense of peace and urgency, as if pressing towards some fulfillment. His intense labor over a written expression of the gospel life for the Friars Minor was now complete: the Holy Rule. He had expressed his mind and established his conviction that it was indeed the Lord himself who had given this to him. Now it was up to the

Friars to do their part and observe what they had promised the Lord. He was called forward.

The signs were clear. No one, least of all Clare, could mistake them. Francis rarely visited San Damiano. When he did, one scarcely knew what to expect. There was that time both Sisters and Friars urged him to come and preach the Word of God to his spiritual daughters. He did. He entered the sanctuary and, with the community assembled, he asked for ashes. Strewing them on his head he recited the penitential Psalm 51: "Miserere mei, Deus." He left without verbal commentary.[54] Indeed, further words would have been superfluous.

But the signs were clear. The end of Saint Francis' earthly pilgrimage was approaching. His body was frail, sick, old, broken, scarcely able to hold the fire of his spirit which kept leaping upward in its hunger for the unseen. He was beginning to resemble that mystical Figure on the Crucifix of San Damiano. His eyes, nearly blind to all on earth, were piercing beyond the pillar of cloud.

The other Brothers came to Clare, especially Francis' early companions, Angelo, Juniper, Philip "the Long," and, less frequently, Leo, because he was usually companion to Francis and his faithful scribe. Was it from them she learned of Francis' intention to retire to Mount Alverna for solitary prayer? The thought of it was almost frightening: the distance was long, the climb steep and arduous, the terrain forbidding. Clare herself would also pray. Somehow she would share this hour with him. She took her station, riveted for long hours at the foot of the crucifix, communing with the mystery of Christ in both his suffering and his triumph. So passed the days of the autumn feasts: the Exaltation of the Cross, the great Solemnity of Holy Michael, the Archangel.

When Francis returned he was totally changed: transformed, transfixed, marked, Christ-ed. There is no mode of measure on earth to gauge the resonance in Clare's soul of the Stigmata on Saint Francis' body: the grief and the joy, the awe, and the wonder that nearly overwhelmed her vulnerable heart. As happens with a woman's devotion, Clare needed to do something. The eloquently tender relic left to us in testimony is the pair of sandals designed and crafted for Francis by the ingenuity of her love, padded in such a way as to relieve the pressure of the body's weight from the painful wounds in his feet from which protruded the bent-back nail points.

Detail of San Damiano Crucifix

Chapter Eight

To place on those who mourn . . .
a diadem instead of ashes . . .
— Isaiah 61:3

Francis was to live another two years. His suffering was intense and he seemed to sense the end drawing near. He desired to return a last time to his beginnings, his call, his first years. And so he came for one last sojourn at San Damiano, staying in a poor little hut, overrun with mice, by the small house where dwelt the Friars who assisted the Sisters of San Damiano. Though he was not totally blind, the affliction of his eyes was severe and the least bit of light from the sun, which formerly had been his comfort and delight, now caused sharp, nearly unbearable pain. So many factors converged, almost collided, to make the depression from which Saint Francis suffered understandable on the natural level. It was God's secret: the work of grace he was bringing to perfection in Francis. What seems wholly inexplicable is the pure burst of sovereign praise that has reverberated through the universe ever since it broke free from that totally unshackled spirit: the Canticle of Brother Sun. This is high mysticism in song (for the sources tell us that Francis also composed the melody and taught it to the Friars), and Clare knew, that as near as the blessed Father was in his hut close by, there was a sense in which he was out of reach to her and the Sisters. She saw his terrible suffering. Though she might be granted by God the power to restore health to her own Sisters by the sign of the Cross, she had no such power where Brother Francis was concerned. He was marked, uniquely so, with the sign of the Cross, and by it his destiny was sealed.

But he was not so distant as to be without compassion for his first and most-loved daughter. No longer were words of exhortation possible or necessary, nor sermons or spiritual talks. Now was his spirit all song. He composed a Canticle also for Clare and her Sisters:

> Listen, little poor ones called by the Lord,
> who have come together
> from many parts and provinces.
> Live always in truth,
> that you may die in obedience.
> Do not look at the life without,
> for that of the Spirit is better.[55]

Then Francis, still singing, urges them to use carefully the alms people give and to care for the sick with great compassion so that they and those who care for them "will be crowned queen[s] in heaven with the Virgin Mary."[56]

Brother Elias, vicar for the Friars in place of their Father Francis, came frequently to San Damiano. Clare shared Francis' confidence in Brother Elias. The unfortunate man was, in fact, capable of greatness, and apparently, as long as he was under the charismatic influence of Blessed Francis, his better side was in command. After Francis' death, however, Elias's second love, "The Lady Politics," would eventually seduce him and then betray him into excommunication from both the Order and the Church. Now, at this point, Elias was devoted to the ailing Saint Francis and wanted him to have the best of medical attention available for his eyes. But the Saint's condition was so poor he could not travel, at least not in the severity of winter.

The parting must have been poignant beyond all other departures for Clare as the warmer weather of late spring permitted travel for the pitiable Brother Francis. The Brothers gathered up that poor, racked body and slowly carried it for the last time down the lane between the budding olive trees. Perhaps the doctors could do something for Francis' eyes.

Clare's eyes lifted to the Figure on the crucifix. The eyes of the Figure there were open wide, gazing into the world of the spirit and, with profound compassion, into Clare's own world, so solitary now.

Though there have been many conjectures, the cause of Saint Clare's own long and serious illness remains unknown. But it began shortly after this time, and one cannot help wondering whether a factor in its onset may have been the removal of the blessed Brother Francis to whom she had always turned for strength and inspiration. While physical causes are one thing, of course, God's purposes are another, and the description of God's ways, given by Saint Paul, is surely evident in the case of the saints: the troubles of this life train us to bear the weight of glory.[57] As the calls of Francis and Clare were so intimately linked and their names were destined to share the same glory, it is not without significance that they should be partners in suffering.

As Francis was being carried about from place to place in the Brothers' vain attempt to find treatment for him, his "little plant" was forced to her bed. In concession to her body's weakness and, doubtless, to the Sisters' pleading, she exchanged the harsh pallet of vine branches for the "luxury" of a straw mattress.[58]

In the meantime, Francis was sensing the approach of "Sister Death" and desired with all the strength of his heart, quite undiminished by the weakness of his body, to return to his beloved Portiuncula, Our Lady of the Angels, cradle of the Brotherhood. So the unthinkably arduous journey back to Assisi began its halting, painful way.

Clare's condition worsened and she began to fear that she would depart this life before her blessed Brother Francis. Totally inconsolable at the thought of never seeing him again, she sent him word. Moved by compassion for this, his first and most-loved daughter, he returned a prophetic word to her grieving heart: "Tell her to put aside all sorrow and sadness because she cannot see me at this moment. But let her know that before she dies both she and her Sisters will see me and have the greatest consolation from me."[59] He also sent her an equally prophetic "last will" which he wrote for her and the Sisters. It would serve her in the future as an anchor of hope and strength and she would enshrine it in her own Rule. "I, little Brother Francis, will to follow the life and poverty of our most high Lord Jesus Christ and of his most holy Mother, and to persevere in them until the end. And I entreat you, my ladies, and give you this counsel: that you live always in this most holy life and poverty. And guard yourselves carefully that you do not ever depart from it in any way on the teaching or advice of anyone."[60]

The long days of the summer of 1226 diminished into autumn as the flame of the mortal life flickered lower in the embers of Francis' body. Then in the late hours of October 3, Sir Brother Sun, setting in a blaze of splendor, looked down for a last glimpse of the bard who had so joyously sung of the deep mystery of his inner secret.

Francis was stretched out upon his Sister Mother Earth, his soul panting in eagerness to leap forward at the touch of the hand of his escort, Sister Death. Then he did leap.

The Little Poor Man who owned nothing now relinquished even his stigmatized body, not without having apologized for the harsh treatment he had meted out to it. Francis had jealously concealed the marks of the wounds, and had done so with relative success. A few of his intimates knew; for the rest, it was only rumored and, since it was a totally unprecedented miracle, the full impact was reserved for this moment when the Saint's lifeless body lay, like a corpus carved of luminous ivory, with the wounds of his Crucified Love exposed now to the view of the whole world.

With that keen sense which characterizes common folk, the people of Assisi had long considered their son and brother Francis not only a Saint, but "the Christ of Umbria." When they came that night to join the Brothers' poignant vigil with the body of father Francis and when they witnessed the marks of the five wounds as divine confirmation about their intuition, a thrill of triumphant joy swept through the crowds. In the morning they bore up that beautiful body on a sea of praise with wave upon wave of song. The body of Saint Francis was carried in jubilation towards the Church of San Giorgio, where it would be laid to rest. But the cortege was held bound to fulfill the promise of the holy Brother Francis to Clare and the Poor Ladies of San Damiano. The procession turned up the lane to the monastery. Francis was returning from life's battle to the Wounded Warrior whose voice from the crucifix had sent him out on the sacred mission: "Go, repair my house."[61] Francis' mission was accomplished.

Brother Thomas of Celano, biographer for Saint Francis, tells the story of this holy farewell. Was he making a subtle implication when he says that the body of Saint Francis, now so identified with that of Christ, was brought to the little opening in the monastic church where the Sisters received the "Sacrament of the Body of the Lord." He continues, "The coffin was opened, in which lay hidden the treasure of supercelestial virtues. . . . Behold, the Lady Clare, who was truly illustrious by the holiness of her merits and was the first mother of the rest since she was the very first plant of this holy Order, came with the rest of her daughters to see their father who would no longer speak to them or return to them but was hastening elsewhere."[62] He goes on to paint in warmest tones the picture of a love so human and yet so exalted, unafraid to give full expression to their feelings for Francis. "Divided between sorrow and joy, they kissed his most radiant hands, adorned with the most precious gems and shining pearls,"[63] the wounds of the stigmata. The crowd which had borne the body of Francis in solemnity and praise to this haven of peace wept in sympathy when they saw the deep sorrow of Clare and the other Poor Ladies.

The cortege drew slowly away and disappeared between the gray, bowing olive trees. San Damiano, always a place of quiet, was now strangely so. The walls seemed strangely unfamiliar, bereft of that which made them real. Instinctively the holy Mother's gaze sought Christ and found his wounded Body on the Cross, pierced yet exalted, lifted up in glory as conqueror of death. Faithfulness would fix her there where Francis had placed her. Deep peace crept in. She knew the eyes of Christ held Francis' soul and gazed upon the Father in the Spirit-embrace that was the Poverello's heaven.

The Madonna
in a Fresco above the Altar
in the Chapel of San Damiano

Chapter Nine

They will be called oaks of justice,
planted by the Lord to show his glory.
— Isaiah 61:3

Though Clare was the "very little plant" of Saint
Francis, the days ahead would demonstrate clearly that
Francis had not been a trellis for a clinging vine, but more
like a stake for a young sapling to grow straight and strong.
Now she stood, fully rooted in poverty and the gospel life,
a symbol and source for those Brothers who came to her,
of fidelity, devotion, and that patience which is a willing-
ness to bear suffering in union with the Crucified Love.

As troubles began to afflict the Friars Minor, Clare was
at her station in prayer and penance. She also took wise
measures among her Sisters to reinforce the treasure of
"holy unity" along with poverty. No records come to us
regarding Clare's influence on the Friars Minor or how
she may have managed to steer a prudent course when
disputes arose over so many things. We do know that she
was a consolation and support to the first companions of
Saint Francis, who often found themselves at variance with
Brother Elias, Saint Francis' successor as general minister of the Friars. But she evidently also maintained confidence in Brother Elias, preferring his advice, as she was to
write to Agnes of Prague, "to the counsels of others and
reckon[ing] it dearer . . . than any gift."[64]

Beatrice, the sister of Clare and Agnes, entered San
Damiano about this time and then also Ortulana, their
pious mother. Requests were coming to the Abbess from

monasteries of Poor Ladies near and far for advice and help in establishing the gospel life of most high poverty in the manner it was observed by Clare and her daughters. To some went Sisters from San Damiano, including her own sister Agnes, who was sent as abbess to Monticello in Florence, and Pacifica, for only a short time, to Valle Gloria in Spello. Then Agnes of Prague, princess of the royal line in Bohemia, refused many offers of marriage, the last a proposal by the Emperor Frederick II, and founded a monastery of Damianites. Five Sisters from Italy went to Prague to form the nucleus of this community.

A deep spiritual friendship developed between Agnes of Prague and Clare of Assisi. Though they never met each other, their kindred spirits gave rise to a fruitful correspondence. Four extant letters of Saint Clare to Agnes are priceless insights into the Saint's soul and revelations of her highly personalized spirituality. Thus we see her writing to Agnes in 1238, four years after Agnes had embraced the gospel life of the Poor Ladies. Clare drew back the veil delicately protecting the depth of her own, now greatly matured, spiritual experience.

Place your mind before the mirror of eternity;
place your soul in the splendor of glory;
place your heart in the likeness of the divine substance,
and transform your entire self into the Image of the
Divinity itself through contemplation.[65]

She promises Agnes that once she definitely dismisses all who in this false and turbulent world ensnare unwary hearts, she will be liberated for the joy to "wholly prefer that One who has surrendered his whole self for your love."[66]

The light within the holy Mother Clare was growing in brilliance in proportion to her ever-increasing fidelity to poverty, her embrace of suffering, her loving compassion for the Sisters, and her selfless prayer. Her biographer relates, "When she returned with joy from holy prayer, she brought from the altar of the Lord burning words that also inflamed the hearts of her Sisters. In fact, they marveled that such sweetness came from her mouth and that her face shone more brilliantly than usual."[67]

There were those who saw her light and marveled at it, admired her, and rejoiced. But only those who caught her fire could begin to understand. Cardinals and popes were to hold the holy Abbess Clare in great esteem and stretch and strain to comprehend her vision, only often to fall short. This was evidenced by their attempts to give assistance to the Poor Ladies whether by arrangements for fixed incomes from lands or legacies which compromised Clare's ideal of most high poverty, or by providing as their form of life a code of law foreign to the spirit of Francis. These were the times and the circumstances for which Saint Francis had prepared her. And she remained faithful. Brother Elias could raise a great, if controversial, basilica to the memory of the blessed father Francis; but for Clare, the holy patriarch lived on in the sacred words and example he had given them.

The energy and application of the holy Abbess at this period are all the more remarkable in consideration of the debilitating state of her health. It was apparently not infrequent for Clare to be unable to rise from her poor bed. Even at such times she valued and responded generously to what she and Francis in their Rules had called "the grace of working."[68] She would have herself propped up with pillows; then she would spin and weave fine cloth for making into altar linens. The Sisters were later to recount how she had made over fifty sets, carefully packing them in specially lined cases and distributing them to the many poor churches in the environs of Assisi.[69]

In her Testament, Saint Clare would state that Saint Francis had left them "very many writings."[70] It is difficult to understand how most of these could have been lost, since very few have come down to us. But even those writings Saint Francis had directed to others, such as his letter to all the faithful, his letter to the Order, and especially his Rule for the Friars Minor, Clare and her Sisters would have cherished as their own patrimony, too.

In his letter to the clergy Saint Francis regrets an apparently common situation: "Let all . . . consider the sad state of the chalices, the corporals, and the altar linens upon which the Body and Blood of our Lord are sacrificed. . . . Well then, let us quickly and firmly amend our ways."[71] Clare's devotion would have received that word as a call to her and her Sisters to do their part. For she would cherish the admonition of Blessed Francis, "Hold back nothing of yourselves for yourselves so that he who gives himself totally to you may receive you totally."[72] Clare would echo this in her letter to Agnes of Prague, "May you feel what his friends feel in tasting the hidden sweetness which God himself has stored up for those who love him. . . . May you wholly prefer that One who has surrendered his whole self for your love."[73]

Possibly it was these two factors, Clare's illness which often confined her to bed and her deep devotion to our Lord in the Holy Eucharist, which occasioned the making of a little oratory where the Blessed Sacrament would be reserved near the dormitory. In the thirteenth century the evolution of Eucharistic piety was not as developed as that which we take for granted. There was as yet no widespread practice of devotion to Jesus' abiding Presence in the reserved Sacrament. But the Holy Spirit led Saint Clare freely, in the intuition of her heart, to abide with the Abiding One.

No matter that her oratory was so very small. It was quite large enough for the One "whom the heavens could not contain."[74] And Clare had the little oratory dedicated in honor of "his own most sweet Mother, who . . . formed him in the tiny cloister of her sacred womb and carried him on her maiden breast."[75] To such dignity did this raise her tiny chapel that Clare did not hesitate a moment to implore no less than six bishops to come to San Damiano for the consecration of that very "minor basilica"! It was to this spot that her heart would so often turn, to the One who was present there to receive her homage, her confidences, and her trust in small or great events.

And there were great events.

The Emperor Frederick II had been arrogantly challenging the papal holdings in central Italy. His troops were marauding and pillaging in the Valley of Spoleto and advancing towards Assisi. San Damiano stood highly vulnerable and defenseless outside the protection of the city walls. Icy fingers of fear tightened their hold on the hearts of the Sisters, and they instinctively turned to their holy Mother who, being sick and unable to rise from her bed, seemed even more pitiably in peril than the others. But she had the heart of a warrior from a family of knights and also the strong trust in Providence of a spiritual family of saints. She told the Sisters she would be their hostage. If the enemy came to San Damiano, they should place her before them. And she meant it!

Then it happened. At about nine o'clock on a Friday morning in September of 1240, a vicious band of Saracen soldiers, mercenaries of Frederick II, stormed the poor little monastery. They were already scaling the walls and dropping down into the cloister when the terrified Sisters ran to Mother Clare. She had herself brought to the door of the refectory; the precious little silver pyx with its "Salutaris Hostia," its "Saving Victim," was brought there also. They would be hostages together, she and her Saving Lord.

She prostrated before Christ in the Sacrament and uttered a prayer that could have come only from the heart of a spouse utterly confident of her position in her Beloved's affection. This prayer, in fact, borders on a challenge. "Look, my Lord, do you wish to deliver into the hands of pagans your defenseless servants whom you have nourished with your own love? Lord, I beg you, defend these your servants whom l am not able to defend at this time."[76] It is from the testimony of Sister Francesca, who had, with Sister Illuminata, been supporting the frail Mother Abbess, that the answer to Clare's prayer comes to us: "A voice of wonderful sweetness [said], 'I will always defend you!' "[77] The witness goes on to say that the holy Mother that evening told the two Sisters who had heard the Voice that they were to tell no one until after her death. When the story was eventually related, the impression must have been great because these words have become the escutcheon of the Order of Saint Clare.

The Saracens were overpowered. They turned about-face and inexplicably retreated. The Lord struck them down by the prayer of a woman.[78]

It is this event that has given rise to the representations of Saint Clare in later centuries that portray her holding a monstrance containing the Blessed Sacrament, sometimes showing the Saracens struck back by the power emanating from the Lord. While this is not historically exact, the symbolism is true and traditional iconography has accorded Saint Clare this privilege of holding up the Holy Eucharist to view.

Less than a year after that crisis, Frederick's full army, under the leadership of the dreaded Vitale d'Aversa, stormed through the Valley of Spoleto, devastating, burning, and pillaging along their way. Then they besieged Assisi. The holy Abbess once more shouldered the weight of the people's defense, enlisting the aid of her "army" of Sisters. Strewing ashes on her bared head and on those of her daughters, she sent them before the Lord to pray that he might have pity on the city that had supported them in their life of worship. The following morning the captain with his army, contrary to his avowed intent to hold out against the city until it would fall to him, lifted camp and left, leaving a stunned population gazing out upon a quiet, peaceful view of a summer's day on the slope of Monte Subasio.

The grateful city and its inhabitants to this day celebrate June 22, the anniversary day, in high festivity. The citizens awake to the sound of silver trumpets, proclaiming the Assisi fanfare from the Civic Tower off the Piazza del Commune. It is *Voto* Day. The red and blue Assisi colors are flown everywhere and medieval costumes recall the day long ago when their favorite daughter became the savior of the "Magnificent City of Assisi."

In the thirteenth century, however, the picture was not all that bright and prospects were frightening. Clare's dear friend on the papal throne, Pope Gregory IX, had been more harassed by Frederick than was San Damiano.

With him it had been a daily suffering, a veritable crown of thorns. Gregory may not always have understood the exalted aspirations of his saintly friends, Francis and Clare, but he did love them well. He had personally taken measures to insure the greater safety of the community of San Damiano. When the Basilica of San Francesco was completed in 1230, the holy relics of the Patriarch were removed from San Giorgio, their first resting-place. San Giorgio remained a hallowed spot for the Order in view of the treasure which had been housed there, so the pope had purchased the site and had construction begun for a monastery and church within the city walls for the Poor Ladies of San Damiano.

One can only guess at the sentiments with which Clare anticipated leaving San Damiano where she had cast the anchor of her soul when Francis had brought her there so many years before. In spite of her deep feeling for this sacred cloister, one notes that, while Clare had no hesitation in expressing her opposition to Pope Gregory's arrangements when they touched upon the essentials, points of absolute poverty and the spiritual ties with the Friars Minor, there is no record of any protest about this proposed move from San Damiano. Since it can scarcely have been less than heart-wrenching for Clare, one of two things may have been in her mind: either she knew that she would die before the move was made by the community, or possibly she was prepared to sacrifice what was unimaginably dear to her, yet not wholly of the essence of her gospel way. San Damiano would be the last full gift of most high poverty.

Santa Maria degli Angeli (Portiuncula)

Chapter Ten

A lasting covenant I will make with them.
— Isaiah 61:8

While Pope Gregory and the people of Assisi were concerned about what might happen to the Sisters in the unprotected San Damiano during those dangerous and troubled times, the holy Mother was more concerned about what might happen to her daughters in the future, when she was no longer on hand to give them guidance and inspiration, and to keep alive for them the counsel of blessed father Francis. Their gospel life of poverty must be committed to writing, and then must be officially approved. Until this would be done, Clare could not rest in the conviction of her mission having been completed. Even Francis had struggled long and hard to achieve this for his Brothers.

If it even occurred to Saint Clare that she was the first woman in thirteen centuries of Christianity to write a Rule of life for religious, she was apparently little impressed by the fact. Her single driving desire was the vocation to which she had been led by the preaching and example of her Father Saint Francis, the true lover and imitator of our Lord Jesus Christ, the vocation to which her daughters had been similarly led.

Various prelates had made well-meant attempts to provide legislation for the communities of Poor Ladies. They had based their Rules on existing codes and practices in other traditions, principally the Benedictine and Cistercian, and by so doing had missed what was so utterly new. These documents were all old wineskins that could not contain this new wine of the spirit that filled Francis and his followers.

As Mother Clare gave expression to the gospel form of life which Blessed Francis had given her, she drew heavily from Francis' own Rule of 1223, which was the basis for the life of the Friars Minor. With the perfect liberty of a faithful follower, totally given to the Spirit of the Lord and his holy manner of working, Clare freely adapted and adjusted Francis' directives to his Brothers in the light of the special needs, experience, and inspiration she and her Sisters recognized as distinctively their own. She also drew from the other legislation given her by ecclesiastics, which she and her daughters had observed for many important, though secondary, elements of monastic life, such as matters regulating enclosure, practices of silence, and the discipline of penance.

But when she would write of poverty, of holy unity, and of that sweetness of charity and courtesy, which should ever characterize the life of the Poor Ladies, it would be more like a song, a holy hymn. She would dip her pen into the well of her heart and write down the words with her own life-blood: "After the most high heavenly Father deigned by his grace to enlighten my heart that I should do penance after the example and teaching of our most blessed Father Saint Francis, I, together with my Sisters, freely promised him obedience a little while after his conversion."[79]

When it was all committed to writing, a sense of peace gathered strength for the holy Abbess, who still had before her the arduous task of gaining the Church's approval. It was a consolation to easily obtain that of the Cardinal Protector, Raynaldus, Bishop of Ostia and

Velletri; but Clare would not rest until the Rule had the seal of the Supreme Pontiff, by this time Pope Innocent IV.

There is a freshness that breathes through the life of Saint Clare. It is evident in her writings; it overflows in her charity among her Sisters; it is undiminished as illness makes its claims upon her physical strength. Even the miracles that are told of her prayer and of the power she called upon with the sign of the Cross are fresh with the freshness of the Spirit who worked in her.

The Holy Spirit seems to have been the operative factor in the miracles her Sisters told of after the death of their Blessed Mother. How else to explain her choice of timing? In the Process of Canonization witnesses testified to the many cures of Sisters by the holy Abbess's sign of the Cross, and when asked how long each Sister had been sick, the answers would vary: "three days," "thirteen months," "eleven years," "six years," "a very long time."[80] Surely the holy Mother had known of her daughters' sufferings all along. What would be the reason, except the prompting of the Spirit of the Lord, for Clare suddenly to take an initiative at some point to heal the suffering Sister?

Though Clare was compassionate and generous in reaching out, even in a miraculous way, to alleviate others, there is no record of her ever benefiting her own frail and pain-racked body. But God would console his bride by a spiritual miracle.

It was Christmas Eve, 1252. Clare was too ill to rise for Matins and go with the other Sisters to the chapel for the beautiful midnight Office of the Nativity of the Lord. There in her infirmary cell, her desolation gave rise to the second of only two prayers directly quoted of Saint

Clare. Once again, direct, familiar, confident in tone, "the Lady then said with a sigh: 'Lord God, look, I have been left here alone with you.' "[81] She then was given to hear most clearly the Christmas services of the Friars at the Basilica of San Francesco, as if she had been there, and to see the crib of the Infant Savior. In her joy and simplicity she told her daughters of this favor the following morning, even chiding in a gentle, almost teasing way, "You left me here alone after going to the chapel to hear Matins, but the Lord has taken good care of me because I was not able to get up from my bed."[82]

Façade of San Rufino

Chapter Eleven

Everlasting joy shall be theirs.
— Isaiah 61:7

The year 1253 dawned. While Clare would not see its close on this earth, it was to be a year of considerable activity for her in spite of her extremely serious illness. Her beloved sister Agnes would return to San Damiano, ending the twenty years and more of their separation.

The Rule. How she longed to see it approved by the Holy Father! Sister Philippa testified in the Process: "Her great desire was to have the Rule of the Order confirmed with a papal bull, to be able one day to place her lips upon the papal seal, and, then, on the following day, to die." Sister Philippa adds, "It occurred just as she desired."[83]

Clare also wrote for the last time to Agnes of Prague in words all of light. If one were to expect a letter of nostalgia or gloomy presentiments, one would not find it here! This letter of a dying woman leaps with joy. The focus of its expression is not the sender and her intense suffering, nor even the "Lady Agnes" to whom it is sent, but rather "the spotless Lamb" to whom each is espoused. Clare calls Agnes "the half of my own soul and the treasury of my heart's singular affection."[84] Towards the end of this letter the holy Mother Clare lets us glimpse into her own heart reflected in the counsel she gives to Agnes: "Contemplating his manifest delights, riches, and unending honors, and then sighing with [your] heart's yearning and love, may you cry out: 'Draw me after you! We shall run in the fragrance of your ointments, O heavenly Spouse! May I run and not lose heart.' "[85]

Not only to Agnes of Prague does Clare reveal the thoughts of her heart. To her own beloved daughters of San Damiano she pours out her maternal attention, intuitively drawing her spiritual nurturing of their vocations to a climax occasioned by the approaching end. As had her father Francis, Clare also had taught the Sisters by word and example. And now she would leave her words to them in writing. She composed a spiritual Testament which stands for all generations of Poor Clares as a sensitive and even passionate revelation of the heart of their Mother, totally possessed by the Spirit of the Lord and given to the love of Christ, her daughters, and the whole Church.

In the spring of that same year the monastery of San Damiano and its holy Abbess were honored by the visit of the Supreme Pontiff, Pope Innocent IV. Cardinal Raynaldo, the Protector of the Order, had come to know, understand, and reverence the blessed Mother Clare and her heroic clinging to the way Saint Francis had taught her and the Poor Ladies. He valued the Rule she had written and he had personally approved it with the authority he had as Cardinal Protector. Too, Raynaldo was a close confidant of Pope Innocent and was anxious to have the Holy Father gain firsthand experience of the eminent sanctity and graciousness of Clare. On April 27, the pope and his entourage arrived in Assisi, and not many days later he paid a visit to San Damiano. It does not take too much stretching of the imagination to guess what Saint Clare spoke about to the Holy Father.

Pope Innocent IV would come once more to the holy Abbess just a few days before her death. Then Saint Clare would give expression to her most profound and humble devotion to the Holy See and to the Church. When the Holy Father offered his hand for the dying Saint to kiss, she begged that she be permitted to kiss his foot also, which she did with greatest reverence. Then "with an angelic expression, she asked the forgiveness of all her sins of the Supreme Pontiff."[86] After remarking that he wished he himself had as little need of pardon as did this holy Mother, "he granted her the gift of perfect absolution and the grace of his fullest blessing."[87]

There was nothing left on earth to shackle her spirit, straining toward its heaven. Surely her pitiable weakened body would offer no resistance. She had often held tryst with Sister Death during the many years of her serious sickness. This time it would be to form a partnership and they would be off.

The summer heat offered little comfort to the sufferer. And she looked for none. Rather, she found untold comfort for her soul in preoccupation with God, whose life and mystery she would so soon share in direct completeness. Grace is essentially identical with glory. Later on, Sister after Sister in the Process of Canonization would claim for Clare the fullness of grace.[88] Now this grace was breaking into the full sun of glory. What comfort may be offered with such a prospect at hand? Indeed, when Brother Raynaldo wished to console the Saint in her sufferings she replied, "After I once came to know the grace of my Lord Jesus Christ through his servant Francis, no pain has been bothersome, no penance too severe, no weakness, dearly beloved Brother, has been hard."[89]

If comfort was needed, it was for those who would be left behind, deprived of "the mirror of the morning star"[90] as they were to call her. As happens at such a time, the secret memories cherished in the heart of each one became companion and comfort through the long vigil.

Sister Pacifica, at Clare's side from the beginning, could recall the very first year at San Damiano and the miracle of the oil. Clare had washed the empty jar herself and set it out for the Brother Questor to replenish. But he found his services quite unneeded when he came for the container. It was full: a symbol of the Holy Spirit, the oil of gladness, flowing and overflowing so freely and unfailingly, anointing with charity the life of the community.

Fresh in the memory of Sister Cecilia was the miracle which took place right in her own hands when, in obedience to her holy Mother, she had cut the only available half-loaf of bread into fifty generous portions to feed the Sisters.

Dear little Sister Francesca cherished the fondest memories of her Mother. It was she who had supported Clare when the Saracens were attacking the monastery and heard a voice "as of a little child [say,] 'I will always defend you.' "[91] Perhaps Sister Francesca had special devotion to the Child Jesus, for she was privileged to see in the lap of her beloved Mother "a young boy who was so beautiful that he could not be described. . . . [She] felt an indescribable sweetness and believed without a doubt he was the Son of God."[92] At another time, when the holy Mother was apparently at the point of death and the priest had brought her Holy Communion, Francesca saw "a great splendor about the head of Mother Saint Clare. It seemed to her the Lord's Body was a very small and beautiful young boy."[93]

Always splendor! Always light! All the memories of

the Sisters gathered about the bedside of their beloved Mother were suffused with light. Sister Agnes of Oportulo had also seen a beautiful boy, who seemed to be about three years old, appear to Saint Clare during the sermon of Brother Philip of Atri. There was a great brilliance around the holy Mother "not like anything material, but like the brilliance of the stars."[94]

There were no stoics in this group gathered about the dying Abbess. The account says, without apology, "the only thing that pleased them, night and day, was crying."[95] Saint Clare's own blood sister, Agnes, not long returned from the monastery of Florence, was "filled with salty tears and begging her sister not to depart and leave her. Clare replied, 'It is pleasing to God that I depart. But stop crying, because you will come to the Lord a short time after me. And the Lord will console you greatly after I have left you.' "[96]

The circle of watchers widened as the word spread that Clare was dying: the papal court, the people of Assisi, the Poor Ladies in the many monasteries which had spread in Italy, Bohemia, Germany, France, Spain, and elsewhere, though only those close-by would know, and of course the Friars Minor. The early companions of Saint Francis, for whom Clare had been a strong support, a consolation, and an inspiration in the difficult years of struggle within the Order of Friars Minor, were there: Brother Angelo, weeping himself, even as he tried to comfort the Sisters; Brother Leo, Francis' "little lamb of God," who could do no more than repeatedly kiss the bed where the Saint lay dying; Brother Juniper, of whom Clare asked what news he had of Christ. Words of fire broke forth from Juniper, telling of his burning love for the Lord.

Clare wished the Brothers to read the Passion of Our

Lord Jesus Christ. A memory was fixed deeply into the soul of Sister Philippa of an event she was bound to keep secret until the Lady Clare had passed from this life. One Good Friday the holy Mother had been so deeply moved by sadness over the Passion and death of Christ that she retired to her cell to spend the sacred time alone in prayer, united to him in his hour of affliction. So profoundly was she absorbed in compassion and contemplation that she was unaware of anything else, whether the passage of time or her need for nourishment. Sister Philippa had, with the most delicate discretion, looked in on her Mother Abbess from time to time. Finally after a night and a day had passed and another night was falling, Sister Philippa roused the holy Mother with the reminder that Father Francis had ordered her not to pass a full day without eating something. As sublime as was her contemplation of Christ who was made obedient even unto death, she did not miss the practical application and returned from her prayer at the call of obedience.[97]

The scene at her deathbed somehow drew together the threads of Clare's whole lifetime. She was deep in communion with the God of her soul, yet she was intensely present to her surroundings, to all gathered at her side, but especially to her daughters. It had been that way throughout forty-two years and it would be that way now as the end approached. She would share even this most intimate time of solitude in God with her community.

Clare spoke softly, "Go in peace, because you will have a good escort. The One who created you has already provided that you will be made holy. The One who created you has infused the Holy Spirit in you and then guarded you as a mother does her littlest child."[98] Sister Anastasia asked the Lady Clare to whom she was speaking. She answered, "I am speaking to my blessed soul."[99] "May you be blessed, O Lord, you who have created my soul!"[100] To dear Sister Amata, Clare's niece, who was alone at her side for some time, the holy Mother kept asking, "Do you see, O child, the King of glory whom I see?"[101] The Sisters also heard their holy Mother Clare speak to the Blessed Trinity in words of such subtlety that they could hardly understand their meaning.[102]

Then a marvelous thing happened. Sister Benvenuta was keeping vigil beside the dying Saint who had, a little over two years before, cured her of a longstanding and extremely painful infection. Now the Sister was grieving over the thought of losing so kind a Mother, yet she "began to think joyfully about the great and wonderful holiness of the Lady Clare."[103] Sister Benvenuta mused about the preparations the whole court of heaven was making to receive her soul, and how "our most glorious lady, the Blessed Virgin Mary, was especially preparing some of her garments for clothing this new Saint."[104] Clare, who from birth had been clothed in a robe of salvation, would soon be wrapped in light as in a robe. Then, through the door of the room which stood slightly ajar, Sister Benvenuta saw a celestial procession of radiant virgins all in white approach the bed of the blessed Mother Clare. The multitude of holy virgins was led by one much more brilliant and far more beautiful than the others, with an appearance beyond description. On her head was a crown, larger than those of the others and formed like a censer, with dazzling light emanating through its apertures, flooding the entire house with a brilliance of unearthly beauty. This wondrous procession came directly to the bed of Saint Clare, where the "Virgin of virgins," whom Sister

Benvenuta believed to be Holy Mary, covered the frail figure of the holy Abbess with a veil of such delicacy that, while Clare was completely covered, still she could be clearly seen through the cloth. Thus, "the body of Clare was covered and the bridal bed was decorated."[105] Then the "Virgin of virgins" bent over the dying Clare and with great tenderness embraced her, drawing her face very near to Clare's so that Sister Benvenuta could not discern the one from the other. Then this blessed entourage departed as it had come, leaving the house once more in darkness.[106]

There was a vague restlessness which alone could explain the lingering of this holy Virgin so ready for the call of the Bridegroom: the Rule. She so desired the ap-

The Death of Saint Clare from a 13th-Century Painting

proval by the Holy Father. At length came a Friar Minor, running the distance from Perugia and the papal court — he had a scroll. Did he not represent the holy Patriarch Francis, whose presence there at this moment completed the scene in a divinely fitting way? And so this herald of the great King brought the good tidings of the gospel way of life shown and taught to Clare by the blessed Father Francis, papally approved, and placed it into her hands. This very document is held today by the daughters of Saint Clare in the protomonastery of Assisi, and in its margin, written in red ink, is the testimony: "Blessed Clare touched and kissed this many times out of devotion."[107]

"Do you see, O child, the King of glory whom I see?"[108] Clare had broken open "the alabaster-jar of her body . . . so that the house of the Church would be filled with the fragrance of her ointments."[109] This she had done faithfully for forty-two years before the blessed gaze of that Crucified One who had told Francis, "Repair my house."[110] Now that same King of Glory looked upon her with love and called her forth. The last words heard from the lips of the dying Mother Saint Clare were, "Precious in the sight of the Lord is the death of his holy ones."[111] The "Lady Clare . . . passed from this life to the Lord, to the clarity of eternal light."[112] It was Monday, August 11, 1253, the feast of Assisi's patron, Saint Rufino.

Composite of the Life of Saint Clare

Chapter Twelve

All who see them shall acknowledge them as a race the
LORD has blessed.
— Isaiah 61:9

Clare's story does not end here. Her desire to have her Rule approved was divinely inspired. She realized that upon this single factor the life to which she had been called would continue. The Church may bury her with honor and devotion — and it did; the Holy Father may even canonize her with great solemnity — and he did. But the *life*! The life would go on. Countless daughters were waiting to be "clothed in the robe of salvation" and follow the Lord in poverty and humility, the gospel life.

In every continent where the Gospel has been preached, the daughters of Saint Clare have brought their gift to the people of God: the cloistered contemplative life of worship, prayer, penance, joy, and love.

> I [Clare] bless you during my life and after my death as much as I am able and even more than I am able, with all the blessings by which the Father of mercies has blessed and will bless his spiritual sons and daughters in heaven and on earth. Amen.

> May the Lord be with you at all times and, wherever you are, may you be with him throughout all time. Amen.[113]

Afterword

Like a bridegroom adorned with a diadem,
like a bride bedecked with her jewels.
— Isaiah 61:10

Reflections on the Prayer and Contemplation
of Saint Clare

Throughout this book telling the life story of Saint Clare, the reality of her prayer and contemplation has been woven through its very texture. This seems most authentic because that is precisely how it was for her. Prayer was the golden thread woven through her life, her "robe of salvation." Prayer was to her noble spirit as breath is to the body. Yet, her gift deserves to be presented more thoroughly to those who are drawn to the beauty of her life and person.

One dimension not developed in the preceding pages is Saint Clare's intimate relationship with Mary, the Mother of God. They lived heart-to-heart. Together they "treasured all these things and reflected on them."[114] Just as Spirit-filled prayer and reflection changes that person truly docile to their transforming power, so the prayer of Clare opened out into an entire mode of being in identification with the Virgin Mary, even in her unique divine motherhood. In a letter to Saint Agnes of Prague, Saint Clare opened this potential to her, and to all of us, recalling that the glorious Virgin of virgins carried Christ within herself — materially, physically. Those who follow in her footsteps, by humility and especially by poverty, also carry him spiritually in their chaste and

105

virginal bodies. This "possession," more secure than any earthly gain, becomes a veritable life.

In the "form of life" which Saint Francis gave Saint Clare and her sisters, he described their Trinitarian call in terms of relationship: "By divine inspiration you have made yourselves daughters and handmaids of the . . . heavenly Father, and have espoused yourselves to the Holy Spirit. . . ."[115] These are precisely Marian positions. And both Francis and Clare would even reverence the soul as "mother" of our Lord Jesus Christ.

Because she with her sisters lived so deep a life of faith at San Damiano, Clare also was blessed for believing the promises of the Lord would be fulfilled in her.

In 1993, Pope John Paul II wrote to the Poor Clares on the occasion of the 800th anniversary of the birth of Saint Clare. His letter describes Clare as "the passionate lover of the poor, crucified Christ, with whom she wants to identify absolutely."[116] The pontiff himself is highly qualified to comment on spirituality. With this statement he singles out the distinctive characteristic of Saint Clare. In her very last letter to Agnes of Prague, when Clare herself was entering the final holocaust of her approaching death, she manifests the fullness of her devotion. Seeing all in a "mirror" placed on the Cross, Clare holds out to her soul sister the promise that by the contemplation of Crucified Love she will "burn ever more strongly with the fire of love."[117] The Blessed Virgin Mary beneath the Cross of Jesus was so identified with his Passion and death that we now hail her as "Queen of Martyrs." Though she did not shed a drop of blood and did not die when Jesus did, the sword of sorrow transfixed her heart. The blessed virgin Clare suffered in like manner and was truly transformed into Christ crucified.

This gifted woman of the 13th century has not left treatises recording the adventure of her contemplative journey of prayer. The same unassuming manner which characterized her life in general marked her profound prayer. Yet, to the heart diligent in pursuit of her limpid spirit, Clare will graciously disclose the outlines of her communion with God.

Her writings are few. Yet, they are replete with glimpses into her transparent soul, disclosing a woman deeply, passionately in love with Jesus Christ. Especially in her letters to Saint Agnes of Prague, she discreetly lifts the veil covering her intimacy with God in the image of a mirror:

> Place yourself before the mirror of eternity.
> Place your soul in the splendor of glory.
> Place your heart within the form of the divine substance,
> and through contemplation transform yourself wholly into the very image of the Godhead![118]

Any woman, gazing into this mirror, seeing herself transformed into beauty beyond all earthly charm or elegance, will be admitted into the very experience of God's intimate friends, that "hidden sweetness God has stored up for those who love Him."[119] This passage links together the classic biblical description of the contemplative experience: "Gustate et videte. . . ." "Taste and see that the Lord is good."[120]

In her correspondence with Saint Agnes, spanning some eighteen years, Clare manifests with consistency her intense focus on the person of Christ and the full flowering of her utter devotion and total gift of herself.

"May you wholly prefer that One who has surrendered his whole self for your love."[121]

What was the experience of her contemporaries? How did they regard the prayer of the Lady Clare?

We are blessed because, although Mother Clare was humble and unassuming, she was in no way secretive. She generously shared herself and her life with her Sisters. They were grateful disciples and faithfully testified in the interviews for the Process of Canonization. Sister Pacifica, who had been close to Clare from the beginning, relates, "The blessed mother was assiduous and careful in her prayers. . . . When she returned from her prayer, the sisters rejoiced as though she had come from heaven."[122] Sister Benvenuta echoes, ". . . Mother Saint Clare was very assiduous, day and night, in prayer . . . her speech was always about the things of God."[123] Sister Amata describes the same and adds: "When she returned from prayer her face appeared clearer and more beautiful than the sun."[124] The testimonies are multiplied, creating an image of a mystic at once fully absorbed in God, and yet open, loving, and compassionate towards the Sisters the Lord had given her. She breathed into their lives the greatest treasure she possessed: God.

But what *was* her prayer? Can we weave together the few facts we know? Do we dare enter the inner chamber of her heart and eavesdrop on the intimacy of her communion with God?

In this biography, we have alluded to some of the external elements that had both an influence on and gave expression to Clare's relationship with Our Lord.

There was the liturgy. It was paramount, and Saint Clare entered deeply into the Church's flow of feasts and fasts. The psalms were her daily bread. The Church prayed them in Latin at that time, and we know by her extant writings that her grasp of Latin was masterful. Her use of Scripture was free and creative; we know her love was passionate.

Therefore she prayed, "How lovely is your dwelling place, O LORD of hosts. . . ."[125] "How lovely . . ."; that is, how delectable. We *taste* in contemplative appreciation and delight, as it were, licking our lips over the very thought of it! "How lovely is your dwelling place," your tenting place, even the Lord Jesus, who described himself as the temple. O Lord! And so the psalms, prayers, readings unfolded to Clare the world of the Spirit. And they unfolded Clare to that world, to be caught up and taken possession of by the Holy Spirit, who was her Spouse.

The extent to which the liturgical prayer absorbed and virtually defined Clare's spirit is shown by the ease with which she burst forth in the words of Psalm 116 as she lay dying: "How can I repay the LORD for his goodness to me? . . . Precious in the eyes of the LORD is the death of his saints."[126]

Even though the formal expression of liturgical prayer and ritual gesture were precious to this daughter of the Church, they in no way overshadowed her exuberant personality. There was an element of spontaneity and familiarity in her manner of speaking to Our Lord from her heart. We know this from the fragments that have been preserved for us of the actual expression of her prayer. In her words to the Lord when the monastery was being stormed by soldiers we clearly note a tone of immense confidence, almost of command: "Look, my Lord, do you wish to deliver into the hands of these pagans your defenseless servants whom You have nourished with Your own love?"[127] One can almost hear the echo of the Virgin

Mary's word to young Jesus, "Son, why have you done this to us?"[128] Clare of Assisi knew him in whom she believed; she counted on his love, which knew her heart through and through.

We have also seen how the prayer of Clare and her Sisters expanded beneath the awesome gaze of the San Damiano Crucifix. Francis long ago had placed Clare there like a vigil light to burn, to be consumed by the flame of Love while casting her brilliant light upon the luminous icon of the Crucified. Jesus looked at her and she looked at him — she looked into him, so that Jesus continued ever to look into Clare. This is contemplation, a life ever growing, every deepening as evidenced in her words to Saint Agnes: "O most noble queen, gaze with affection, consider with attention, contemplate with love"[129] that communion with Christ, who is looking into one's soul, aware of his very presence in her heart.

Clare used the image of a mirror as more than a figure of speech. We clearly see it manifest in her life. She gazed into what she called this "Mirror, hung on the wood of the Cross,"[130] contemplating both Jesus and her inner self. Clare did this so faithfully and with such deep love that she truly came to identify with the poor, crucified Christ absolutely. In fact, so complete was her union with him that her Sisters recalled the story of a particular Thursday in Holy Week. The "Legend" tells of the occurrence of her prayer in this way:

> While in her own prayer she was accompanying the praying Savior and when saddened even to death she experienced the effect of his sadness, she was filled at once with the memory of his

capture and of the whole mockery, and she sank down on her bed.[131]

She remained so completely absorbed in the passion of Our Lord that she was unaware of the passage of time for a night and a day.[132] Such was the intensity of her prayer and contemplation.

The result of such a life, unfolding in faithful, persevering, and assiduous prayer, was a profound conformity to Christ. So absorbed was Clare in Christ that before her death she reflected Jesus' interior movements as revealed in Saint John's Gospel in the section preceding the passion narrative. Clare on her deathbed asked that the Gospel be read. Then she began to speak "so softly the sisters were not able to understand her well,"[133] reports Sister Philippa, third witness in the Process. Again, like Christ's Mother, Clare was wrapped in silence. And like Christ himself, her communion before death was with the Blessed Trinity. "She said many things about the Trinity. . . ."[134] We may end this reflection, then, with the summary given to us by Pope John Paul II in his letter about Saint Clare:

Thus the hard bed of the Cross becomes the sweet nuptial bed and the life-long recluse of love finds the most passionate accents of the beloved in the Song of Songs: "Draw me after you . . . O heavenly Spouse." Clare experiences the purest joy experienced by any creature: the joy of living in Christ the perfect union of the three divine Persons, entering as it were into the ineffable circuit of Trinitarian love.[135]

And Clare fulfills perfectly the "form of life," the Trinitarian call, given her by Saint Francis.

To the praise of our Lord Jesus Christ
who lives and reigns
with the Father and the Holy Spirit
forever and ever.[136]
Amen.

Epilogue

I am frequently impressed by the relevance of Clare of Assisi not only as a woman for her own time but also for us today. She was the one who, like Mary, placed herself at the disposal of God and believed that she would attain salvation as long as she cooperated entirely with this God, who loved her without reservation. What does she teach us?

She exhorts her sisters to "pray always with a pure heart . . . in humility and with patience." If prayer is to become our life so that we pray always, our hearts need to be pure, i.e., totally given to God. We need to grow into a kind of single-heartedness so that God has priority in all we do. The focus of our lives is always on the things of God. This is where we should live although in actuality we know this often does not seem to be the case. As we move from one situation to another, our attention ebbs and flows; ultimately, we come to rest in the direction of our deepest desiring. The big question we must face is where that desiring truly is.

Clare reminds us that we need humility and patience in our life of prayer and relationship with God. Humility opens us to truth, putting everything into true perspective: who God is, who we are, the preciousness of each individual, the grace that lies hidden everywhere. This happens only if we are patient, if we accept the Cross that will mark every life caught up in the paschal mystery as well as the nothing that will be the staple of most of our prayer.

As prayer becomes the directional force in our life and as we grow in humble self-acceptance, we become better able to name the sinful tendencies that pull at us and then to turn from them more quickly. We are less upset by this experience of our own weakness and more appreciative of God's faithful love. Our focus begins to shift from self at center stage to a sustained thrust toward God and the things of God. Our life bears the fruit of "praying always."

Such a focused life is the climate of prayer, that air which we breathe in God's spirit. But sustaining such a life of prayer presupposes that times of explicit prayer have a certain priority in our life. They did for Clare as for all the saints. Her days were patterned by the regular rhythm of the liturgy, both the Eucharist and the Liturgy of the Hours. It was a strong daily diet, rich in the word of God where many hours given to prayer nourished her spirit. However, the amount of time she gave to prayer is less important than her dedication. It is quite possible to make a substantial investment in times for prayer without really being there. We are only being dutiful or compulsive. The saints were present to God in their devotion. Clare gave herself the gift of time for prayer; her heart's devotion demanded it.

Who will be the Clare and Francis of Assisi for our own time and century? The Church and the Order have a right to expect that each one of us should be numbered in their company.

— Father Kurt Hartrich, O.F.M.

Chronology of the Life of
Saint Clare of Assisi

1194   Birth of Clare

1212
  March 18   Clothing of Clare at the Portiuncula.
  April 3   Clare is joined by her sister Catherine;
                Francis clothes her and gives her the
                name Agnes.
  May   The two sisters are brought to San
                Damiano by Francis.

1215   Clare becomes Abbess of the community
                of Poor Ladies.

1215-16   Privilege of Poverty given by Pope Inno-
                cent III.

1219   Agnes is sent as Abbess to Montecelli near
                Florence.

1224-25   Beginning of Clare's illness; Francis re-
                ceives the Stigmata.

1226
  Sept-Oct   Francis sends last will to Sisters;
                death of Francis.

1234-53   Letters of Clare to Agnes of Prague.

1240	Repelling of Saracens.
1241	Liberation of Assisi through Clare's prayers.
1252 Dec	Approval of Rule by Cardinal Rainaldo Clare's Christmas Eve vision.
1253	Testament of Clare. Return of Agnes to San Damiano.
April	Visit of Pope Innocent IV to Clare.
Aug 9	Pope Innocent approves Clare's Rule in the Bull *Solet Annuere*.
Aug 11	Death of Clare.
Oct 18	Opening of Process of Canonization.
1255	
Aug 15	Canonization of Saint Clare by Pope Alexander IV.

Notes

1. Confraternity of Christian Doctrine, *New American Bible*, Is 61:10, Thomas Nelson Publishers, 1971. [Hereafter, NAB.]
2. Fourth Letter to Saint Agnes of Prague, 15-18, author's translation.
3. NAB, Ps 104:2, op. cit.
4. NAB, Jn 12:8, op. cit.
5. Alfred Lord Tennyson, *The Brook.*
6. Early sources do not agree on the date of Clare's birth. It was either in 1193 or 1194, more likely the latter.
7. This may have been the bishop's cathedral of Santa Maria Maggiore. The baptismal font, now in San Rufino and clearly identified as the font at which Francis and Clare were baptized, was possibly still in Santa Maria Maggiore at that date awaiting the completion of the construction of San Rufino.
8. Regis J. Armstrong, O.F.M. Cap., *Clare of Assisi: Early Documents*, "Legend of Saint Clare," 2, Paulist Press, 1988.
9. Ibid., Preface.
10. Ibid., 3.
11. Loc. cit.
12. Ibid., 4.
13. Marion A. Habig, O.F.M., ed. *Saint Francis of Assisi: Omnibus of Sources*, Celano, "Second Life," VI:10, Franciscan Herald Press, 1973.
14. Mother Mary Francis, P.C.C., *Rule and Testament of Saint Clare*, p. 34, Franciscan Herald Press, 1987.

15. Cf. Armstrong, "Process of Canonization," 5:2; 11:5, op. cit. [Hereafter, "Process."]
16. Ibid., "Legend of Saint Clare," 5.
17. Mother Mary Francis, P.C.C., op. cit., p. 33.
18. Cf. Armstrong, "Legend of Saint Clare," 7, op. cit.; NAB, Heb 13:13, op. cit.
19. Armstrong, "Process," 13:1, op. cit.
20. Second Letter to Saint Agnes of Prague, 12-13, author's translation.
21. First Letter to Saint Agnes of Prague, 7, 9, 14, author's translation.
22. Ibid., 12.
23. Cf. NAB, Ex 14:25, op. cit.
24. Armstrong, "Legend of Saint Clare," 24, op. cit.
25. Ibid., 25.
26. Loc. cit.
27. Loc. cit.
28. Ibid., 26.
29. Loc. cit.
30. Loc. cit.
31. Ibid., 10.
32. Mother Mary Francis, P.C.C., op. cit., p. 25; Regis Armstrong, O.F.M., and Ignatius C. Brady, O.F.M., *Francis and Clare, the Complete Works,* "The Later Rule" V:l, Paulist Press, 1982.
33. Armstrong, "Legend of Saint Clare," 10, op. cit.
34. Mother Mary Francis, P.C.C., op. cit., p. 34.
35. Mother Mary Francis, P.C.C., op. cit., p. 17.
36. Cf. Ibid., p. 26.
37. Armstrong, "Process," 1:6, op. cit.
38. Mother Mary Francis, P.C.C., op. cit., p. 25.
39. Habig, "Legend of the Three Companions," 14, op. cit.

40. Cf. Armstrong, "Process," 1:8, op. cit.

41. Loc. cit.

42. Third Letter to Saint Agnes of Prague, 38-40, author's translation.

43. Cf. Armstrong, "Process," 1:12; 2:16; 3:7; 4:3; 8:3; 11:1; 13:3, op. cit.

44. Ibid., 8

45. Cf. Armstrong, "The Privilege of Poverty of Pope Innocent III," Introduction, op. cit.

46. Armstrong, "Legend of Saint Clare," 14, op. cit.

47. Loc. cit.

48. Ibid., 37.

49. Loc. cit.

50. Cf. Armstrong, "Process," 6:6 and 7:2, op. cit.

51. Mother Mary Francis, P.C.C., op. cit., p. 36.

52. Armstrong/Brady, "Letter to the Entire Order," 27, op. cit.

53. Mother Mary Francis, P.C.C., op. cit. p. 36.

54. Habig, Celano, "Second Life," 207.

55. Armstrong, "Canticle of Exhortation," 1-3, op. cit.

56. Ibid., 6.

57. Cf. NAB, cf. 2 Cor 4:17, op. cit.

58. Armstrong, "Legend of Saint Clare," 17, op. cit.

59. Armstrong, "Assisi Compilation," 109, op. cit.

60. Mother Mary Francis, P.C.C., op. cit., p. 17.

61. Habig, Celano, "Second Life," VI:l0, op. cit.

62. Ibid., Celano, "First Life," 116.

63. Ibid., 117.

64. Second Letter to Saint Agnes of Prague, 16, author's translation.

65. Third Letter to Saint Agnes of Prague, 12, 13, author's translation.

66. Ibid., 15.

67. Armstrong, "Legend of Saint Clare," 20, op. cit.

68. Mother Mary Francis, P.C.C., op. cit., p. 19.

69. Cf. Armstrong, "Legend of Saint Clare," 28;
    Process, 1:11, 6:14.

70. Mother Mary Francis, P.C.C., op. cit., p. 35.

71. Armstrong/Brady, "Letter to the Clergy," 4, 10, op.
    cit.

72. Ibid., "Letter to the Entire Order," 29, op. cit.

73. Third Letter to Saint Agnes of Prague, 14-15, auth-
    or's translation.

74. Ibid., 18.

75. Ibid., 18-19.

76. Armstrong, "Legend of Saint Clare," 22, op. cit.

77. Armstrong, "Process," 9:2, op. cit.

78. NAB, cf. Jdt 13:4-9, op. cit.

79. Mother Mary Francis, P.C.C., op. cit., p. 17.

80. Armstrong, "Process," 1:16; 2:13, 16; 3:10, 11; 4:7-
    10; 7:12, 13 and others, op. cit.

81. Ibid., 3:30.

82. Ibid., 7:9.

83. Ibid., 3:32.

84. Fourth Letter to Saint Agnes of Prague, 1, author's
    translation.

85. Ibid., 28-31; NAB, cf. Sg 1:3, op. cit.

86. Armstrong, "Legend of Saint Clare," 42, op. cit.

87. Loc. cit.

88. Cf. Armstrong, "Process," 3:2; 6:5; 7:11; 10:2; 11:4;
    14:4, op. cit.

89. Ibid., "Legend of Saint Clare," 44.

90. Ibid., "Notification of Death."

91. Ibid., "Legend of Saint Clare," 22; Process, 9:2.

92. Ibid., "Process," 9:4.

93. Ibid., 9:10.

94. Ibid., 10:8.
95. Ibid., "Legend of Saint Clare," 43.
96. Loc. cit.
97. Cf. Ibid., 31; "Process," 3:25.
98. Ibid., "Process," 11:3.
99. Loc. cit.
100. Ibid., "Legend of Saint Clare," 46.
101. Loc. cit.; cf. "Process," 4:19.
102. Cf. Ibid., "Process," 14:7.
103. Ibid. 11:4.
104. Loc. cit.
105. Ibid., "Legend of Saint Clare," 46.
106. Cf. Ibid., "Process," 11:4.
107. Ibid., "Introduction to Rule," p. 60.
108. Ibid., "Legend of Saint Clare," 46.
109. Ibid., 10.
110. Habig, Celano, "Second Life" VI:l0, op. cit.
111. Armstrong, "Process," 10:10, op. cit.; NAB, Ps 115:15, op. cit.
112. Ibid., "Process," 3:32.
113. Mother Mary Francis, P.C.C., op. cit., p. 41.
114. NAB, Lk 2:19, op. cit.
115. Mother Mary Francis, P.C.C., op. cit. p. 17.
116. Pope John Paul II, "Clare Identified With the Poor Christ," 4, 1993.
117. Ibid.
118. Third Letter to Saint Agnes of Prague, 12-13, author's translation.
119. Ibid., 14.
120. NAB, Ps 34:9a, op. cit.
121. Third Letter to Saint Agnes of Prague, 15, author's translation
122. Armstrong, "Process," 1:9, op. cit.

123. Ibid., 2:9, 10.
124. Ibid., 4:4.
125. NAB, Ps 84:2, op. cit.
126. Ibid., Ps 116:12, 15.
127. Armstrong, "Legend of Saint Clare," 22, op. cit.
128. NAB, Lk 2:48, op. cit.
129. Second Letter to Saint Agnes of Prague, 20, author's translation.
130. Fourth Letter to Saint Agnes of Prague, 24, author's translation.
131. Armstrong, "Legend of Saint Clare," 31, op. cit.
132. Cf. loc. cit.
133. Armstrong, "Process," 3:20, op. cit.
134. Loc. cit.
135. Pope John Paul II, 5, op. cit.
136. Armstrong, "Legend of Saint Clare," 62, op. cit.

About the Author

Sister Mary St. Paul, P.C.C., has been a member of the Poor Clares for more than forty years. She has served as infirmarian, novice mistress, and the Mother Superior of the monastery of Poor Clares in Cleveland.

Other Books About Saints

Faces of Holiness by Ann Ball. The faces and stories of 175 twentieth-century saints and martyrs come to vivid life. 0-87973-**950**-9, paper, $14.95, 272 pp. 0-87973-**919**-7, Poster, 18" x 24", $3.95.

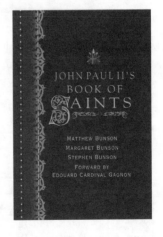

John Paul II's Book of Saints, Matthew Bunson, Margaret Bunson, Stephen Bunson. Extensive biographies of the saints and blesseds named by Pope John Paul II during his pontificate. 0-87973-**934**-7, hardcover, $19.95, 384 pp.

Our Sunday Visitor

*Your Source for Discovering
the Riches of the Catholic Faith*

Our Sunday Visitor has an extensive line of materials for young children, teens, and adults. Our books, Bibles, booklets, CD-ROMs, audiocassettes, and videos are available in bookstores worldwide.

To receive a FREE full-line catalog, or for more information, call **Our Sunday Visitor** at **1-800-348-2440**. Or write: **Our Sunday Visitor**, 200 Noll Plaza, Huntington, IN 46750.

- -

❑ Please send me a catalog.

Please send me material on:

❑ Apologetics/Catechetics   ❑ Reference works
❑ Prayer books   ❑ Heritage and the saints
❑ The family   ❑ The parish

Name _____
Address _____
City _____ ST _____ Zip_____
Telephone (____)_____

AO3BBABP

- -

❑ Please send a friend a catalog.

Please send a friend material on:

❑ Apologetics/Catechetics   ❑ Reference works
❑ Prayer books   ❑ Heritage and the saints
❑ The family   ❑ The parish

Name _____
Address _____
City _____ ST _____ Zip_____
Telephone (____)_____

AO3BBABP

- -

OUR
SUNDAY
VISITOR
BOOKS

Our Sunday Visitor
200 Noll Plaza
Huntington, IN 46750
1-800-348-2440
E-mail us at: osvbooks@osv.com
Visit us on the Web: http://www.osv.com

Your source for discovering the riches of the Catholic Faith